THE HERALD DIARY

Twisted Tails & Nut Jobs

Lorne Jackson

BLACK & WHITE PUBLISHING

First published 2021
by Black & White Publishing Ltd
Nautical House, 104 Commercial Street
Edinburgh, EH6 6NF

1 3 5 7 9 10 8 6 4 2   21 22 23 24

ISBN: 978 1 78530 366 1

The publisher has made every reasonable effort to contact copyright holders of images in this
book. Any errors are inadvertent and anyone who for any reason has not been contacted is
invited to write to the publisher so that a full acknowledgement can be made in subsequent
editions of this work.

A CIP catalogue record for this book is available from the British Library.

Typeset by www.creativelink.tv
Printed and bound by Clays Ltd, Elcograf S.p.A.

Contents

Introduction

THE Times They Are A-Changin' sang Bob Dylan. Though if the troubadour had been busking in Scotland in the last year or so he may have swapped those triumphant words for the more circumspect: "Wit's Goin' On?" We live in an era where Zoom calls replace handshakes and hugs. Where nights on the tiles give way to Netflix and nibbles on the sofa. Where pupils skip school . . . on the advice of their teachers.

The Herald Diary has chronicled these topsy-turvy times, while also taking our readers' minds off the merry-go-round of madness with our branded blend of funny anecdotes and cockamamie comments. In other words, Wit's Going On within these very pages? Wit and other forms of humour.

So crack open a bottle of something fizzy, crack open the following pages and crack yourself up with our latest collection of wacky, warped and wondrous tales.

1
What a Tiddly Wee Hingmy

AND so the year 2021 proved to be everything we all hoped it would be. A return to normality, freedom from fear, restrictions eradicated and . . .

Wait. Sorry. Scrap that. We're really not sure how the above paragraph sneaked into the editorial process. It must be from a draft chapter of this book, written by the Diary team in the early hours of the first of January 2021, back when everything seemed more positive as our minds were fogged by that fourth magnum of Hogmanay Champagne.

In truth, 2021 turned out to be something of a 2020 reboot. The same plot, the same cast. Though a bigger budget and wilder special effects. In other words, there was to be no balm from the bampottery of the year before. The crazy stuff just kept crazying.

Donald remained President for a few more months, which meant more tiffs and tantrums from the tangerine-tinted bloke with the trapdoor hair. Covid stood its ground too, though a vaccine was on its way.

The Scottish public faced further dangers and restraints on their freedom, though our upbeat Diary contributors continued to supply us with humour in between the hammer blows.

So, here's our lowdown on lockdown . . .

IN her nineties and living in a Glasgow care home, Moyna Gardner sent the following evocative verse to her relatives instead of a card last Christmas. It was, of course, written during a lockdown Yuletide . . .

> *"We'll have our Christmas on the phone*
> *Which does not suit this deaf old crone*
> *So eat and drink and laugh and browse*
> *As much as government allows*
> *And I will sit here on the shelf*
> *Singing carols by myself*

Anything they serve I'll guzzle
Working on my crossword puzzle
I might even quite out-booze you all
If Laithwaites just supply my usual."

AN unlikely story from a reader who assures us that he watched a panto where the crowd screamed: "He's two metres behind you!"

IT'S been a difficult year for most, though reader Ted Jones isn't complaining. "The whole mask-wearing thing has really propelled my career as a ventriloquist," he says.

EXHAUSTED reader Alan Doyle gets in touch in the early hours of the first of January. And this is what he has to say: "After a year of fighting 2020, I can finally declare . . . 2021."

AN optimistic Milngavie reader finds himself planning his holidays at the start of 2021. "I hope to make Iceland in February," he says. "If that goes well, I may look at Asda in March followed by Tesco in April."

THE son of reader Rachel Benson is strict and regimented when it comes to tackling the work set by his school to be completed at home during lockdown.

He wakes early in the afternoon and doesn't learn any English. He then takes a lunch break, after which he refuses to tackle maths. In the afternoon and evening he dodges physics, chemistry, biology and French. Then it's early to bed (11.55 p.m.), so he can repeat the process the following day.

"With this work ethic he'll eventually be awarded a PhD in skiving," predicts Rachel.

AFTER almost a year of lockdown, reader Norrie Johnstone has one bitter regret about his actions preceding the momentous event: "Had I known in March that it was the last time I'd be in a restaurant," he says, "I would have ordered dessert."

THRILL-seeking reader Lisa Hannah had high hopes for 2021, looking forward to nights out, constant socialising and escapades in exotic locations. Such ambitions have been severely curtailed.

She now claims her journey from 2021 hoper to 2021 moper is like receiving an unexpected package from Amazon. She describes the process thus:

"Ooh! Huge, exciting box! Is it for me? Yippee! Must tear it open . . .

Oh.

What a tiddly wee hingmy inside. Still, gotta love that excess packaging . . ."

IN an attempt to lighten the mood during murky times, the Diary is compiling a social distancing playlist. Top tunes suggested include 'From a Distance', made famous by the wonderful Nanci Griffith, who sadly died this year. Also Dionne Warwick's 'Walk On By'.

THE wife of reader Bob Jamieson was explaining to the couple's eleven-year-old granddaughter, Amelie, that Bob couldn't celebrate his birthday in a restaurant as all dining establishments were closed because of lockdown.

The little girl was then informed that a booking would be made as soon as eateries opened up.

"Will it be a posh one?" enquired Amelie eagerly. "One with lots of Michelangelo stars?"

A WIDOWED Edinburgh pensioner was outlining his activity regime to his granddaughter, explaining that when he went for a walk with a lady friend they always took the necessary precautions.

The granddaughter raised a startled eyebrow, forcing the senior citizen to add: "You know, social distancing."

FALKIRK Council were keen to hear about local people's travel habits since the pandemic began and offered the chance to win shopping vouchers to those who completed a survey on the subject.

A resident of the town told us he could easily describe his far-flung journeys in a few brief words:

"Voyage to the end of the living room. Quest to the kitchen. Expedition upstairs. Bed. Repeat indefinitely."

MORE from our social distancing playlist. For your listening predilection, we suggest . . . Fleetwood Mac's 'Go Your Own Way'.

BEING trapped at home has forced many people to get creative. Some bake bread. Others learn a musical instrument. Meanwhile, proud reader Steve Doyle says: "I managed to make dandruff from scratch."

A LINGUISTICALLY limber reader asks the pertinent question: "Are we locked down or up?"

WITH Masonic lodges being used as vaccinating centres, Hugh Dougherty wonders if chaps will now have to roll up a trouser leg to receive their jag.

AN unlikely tale from a reader who assures us he spotted a bloke at the Barras selling coronavirus vaccines.

"It was two pounds for an Oxford or three for a Pfizer," he reports.

A DELIGHTED Malcolm Boyd from Milngavie visited his local sports centre to receive a jab in an upper limb as part of the vaccination programme. With the Scottish government struggling to keep up with the English roll-out, Malcolm is curious to know who will win this particular 'arms' race.

(At least, for once, it won't be the Yanks or Russians.)

ANOTHER musical number for our social distancing playlist. Reader Graham Richmond suggests 'You Can Look (But You Can't Touch)', a song associated with the Bella Twins, two sisters who gained fame in America through their fighting prowess on the wrestling circuit. (Think Big Daddy and Giant Haystacks. Only slightly more sylph-like.)

DIARY readers are usually sharp as tacks, specifically those tacks that find their way onto a bare foot when one is stumbling around in search of the bathroom at 2.30 in the morning.

Unfortunately, lockdown has mind-mushing properties which affect even the most astute of our correspondents.

"I woke up yesterday," sighs reader Joe Knox, "and I couldn't remember whether it was Pancake Tuesday or Sheffield Wednesday."

SOCIAL distancing playlist . . . continued. Ian Lyell from Mauchline claims one of the most obvious songs to include is 'The Bonnie Banks o' Loch Lomond', which includes a commendable edict that even Chris Whitty would approve of: "Ye'll tak' the high road an' I'll tak' the low road . . ."

MOST folk are discombobulated by the long lockdown nights, which often become a toss-and-turnathon for people struggling with stress-induced insomnia.

Early in January, the Glasgow-based theatre impresario, Robert C. Kelly, suggests we should all look on the bright side, adding: "Only six more sleeps till Christmas."

TWO more musical numbers to add to our social distancing playlist . . .

'Behind the Mask' by Fleetwood Mac.

'Step Inside Love' (and you'll get a visit from the polis) by Cilla Black.

LOVE means never having to say you're sorry. It also means getting jabbed in the arm with a pointy implement, first thing in the morning. At least it does for Moira Love (yup, that's her real name) from Cumbernauld, who informs us that she and her husband are booked to get their coronavirus vaccines at 8.15 a.m. on Sunday 14 February, an auspicious day in any lovey-dovey's diary.

The appointment means there will be no petal-strewn breakfast in bed.

"Though maybe we'll be offered chocolates and a glass of Bucks Fizz on arrival at the vaccine centre," says Moira, who is as much an optimist as she is a romantic.

WITH cafés and restaurants shut and home visits frowned upon, socialising is a lost art during lockdown. Though not completely.

A reader strolled past a couple of refined elderly neighbours in Newton Mearns, chatting outside one of their houses while enjoying cups of hot chocolate and a plate of Jaffa Cakes.

With no table, they balanced the food and drink on a grey plastic wheelie bin. "It was very la-di-da in a trashy sort of way," chuckles our reader.

IN a moment of deep and profound contemplation, one of our readers says: "If the government agreed to put the vaccine into beer, then opened all the pubs, we would all be vaccinated by the weekend."

True.

Though we'd all be too sloshed to notice.

Back to the drawing board . . .

WE continue providing a valuable public service by devising more efficient methods of rolling out the coronavirus vaccine. Reader Gordon Philips suggests the government should allow Amazon delivery drivers to administer it, adding: "The entire population would be immunised in twenty-four hours flat. Or one hour flat, for those with Prime."

CELTIC manage to skip the UK-wide lockdown by arranging a training trip to Dubai. Reader Barry Moore wonders if it would be equally acceptable if he jets abroad to improve his own ball-playing skills.

"Though I'll be using a beachball," he concedes.

INVALUABLE advice from Irish comedian Michael Redmond, who is based in Glasgow's West End. He says: "Break the boredom of lockdown by standing on your ironing board and imagine you're surfing down a 200-foot wave crashing towards the shoreline."

HAVING received his vaccination in Haddington last week, reader Mike Wilson wonders how his favourite cartoon character would have responded after getting his injection.

He concludes that Fred Flintstone would rush round Bedrock City shouting: "Jabba-dabba-doo."

CURIOUS reader Bert Marshall asks: "Once everybody in the UK has been injected, will we be a vacci nation?"

ANOTHER story focusing on how our readers are faring in uncertain times. Mitch Jones tells us about a text message received from a friend, which read: "Quick update about how I'm doing: Aaaaaaaaaaargh! So, how's yerself?"

Mitch tells us: "I was very impressed by my pal's mental resilience during such a bleak period. If that had been me sending that text, I'd have put loads more a's in the Aaaaaaaaaaargh."

CONTEMPLATIVE Bob Wallace from Pollokshields is mulling over the important lessons he's garnered from the last few extraordinary months.

1) He learned that Pfizer has a silent P.
2) He learned how to master a silent P when his wife is on a Zoom business call.

IN an effort to make the best of being confined to quarters, David Donaldson decides to grow his own potatoes. Instructions say to 'chit' them by letting them sprout near a window.

As David is arranging the seed potatoes in old egg boxes, he overhears his wife explaining to a friend on the phone: "David's busy chibbing the potatoes."

"After months of lockdown, no Glasgow jury would convict me," shrugs David.

A FRIEND of Stevie Campbell from Hamilton spent lockdown working from home as an agoraphobia counsellor.

"He tells me it's been really quiet," adds Stevie. "I wonder why?"

WATCHING television, Ken McLean from Denny enjoyed the STV drama *Too Close*. "I look forward to the pandemic-based sequel called *Not Too Close*," he adds.

THE wife of reader Jack Davidson is delighted she has an appointment for her first coronavirus vaccine, though she hates spiky objects and is rather trepidatious about receiving the injection.

"Which arm do they jag you in?" she nervously asked her husband, who has already received his vaccine.

"Does it matter?" he replied. "Which arm would you prefer?"

"Somebody else's," she admitted.

GLASGOW crime writer Graeme Macrae Burnet is a talented scribbler, though he is itching to prove he also has exceptional entrepreneurial skills.

"I'm thinking of opening a pub called The Vaccinated Arms," he reveals.

CELEBRITY hairdresser Denise McAdam, who is Scottish though based in London, has been volunteering at a vaccine centre where she asked a chap: "Had a jag yet?"

"No," replied the fellow.

Though he added that he once owned a Merc.

RETAIL roars back into action after yet another lockdown, and Glasgow comedian Johnny Mac is thrilled.

"Another step towards normality; the shoplifters can go back to work," he says, adding sympathetically, "it's been a tough time for them."

WITH lockdown eased, Jason Cantrell finds himself on a train to Glasgow Central, where a conductor demands to see his ticket. Our reader is astonished. As a key worker, he has hopped on and off many trains during this period, and not once has an official asked for a ticket.

A chap in a nearby seat is equally taken aback by this exotic occurrence, and chuckles dryly to the conductor. "So now yer wantin' us tae pay for oor jaunts on yer trains?" says he. "Wit ever next?"

WHO needs logic, rational thought and concerns about health when you can swap such fripperies for a pinch of baccy tightly wrapped in a sliver of paper?

Reader Alan McKinney tells us: "Just witnessed a bloke pulling down his Covid mask to puff on a cigarette. Einstein-levels of genius emanating from that one."

STROLLING down Sauchiehall Street, reader Cynthia Arnold spotted a teenage girl dressed in the timeless punk fashion of spiky hair and shredded jeans.

The sartorial elegance of this rough-n-tumble rebel was topped off by a T-shirt emblazoned with one word in suitably defiant lettering, which snarled: DISOBEY!!!

She also happened to have a face mask neatly strapped to her face.

"Talk about mixed messages," chuckles Cynthia.

"I ASKED my husband how we should celebrate when lockdown is finally over for good," says reader Jennifer Beattie.

Hubby's answer? "How about a nice night in?"

A NIPPY remark. Nick Vargg from King's Park was about to receive his Covid vaccination at Castlemilk Sports Centre when the male nurse treating him spotted the Berwick Rangers tattoo on his patient's left arm.

In an unhappy tone of voice the nurse said: "They beat Glasgow Rangers in 1967, didn't they?"

The medical chap, who we're guessing likes to drape himself in blue apparel of a Saturday afternoon, proceeded to give Nick his jab.

After the procedure was over the nurse said, with a fair amount of relish: "Enjoy yer sair arm."

"It seems that fifty-four years of hurt hasn't softened the average Glasgow Rangers fan," chuckles Nick, who was amused to be needled while getting his needle.

RECEIVING a Covid injection in Austria can be a jarring experience, reveals reader Richard Davis who lives in the central European nation.

He tells us that the standard greeting from the person administering the jab is "Grüß Gott", which can be translated as the rather disconcerting: "Greet God."

Presumably the standard reply to such a statement is: "I'm afraid I've got a rather jam-packed schedule down here on earth. So I'll have to decline that appointment, thank you very much."

OBSERVANT reader Hugh Peebles is intrigued by the logo splashed across Borders Buses, which sweetly states: "Bringing people together." Hugh concedes that this is a fine sentiment, though he wonders if it's a tad touchy-feely with social distancing rules in place.

Perhaps the bus company slogan could be changed to: "Bringing people together until they get just a little too close, then screeching: 'Halt right there. Back up, buddy. Back up, we said! Don't move till we fetch a tape measure to check for that two metre gap.'"

A QUALITY question from reader Jay Yuille, who asks: "Do naturists have to wear masks?"

The Diary believes they do.

Though only on their faces.

CHATTING to an old seafaring chum about lockdown, a Milngavie reader agreed with this fellow that the situation was similar to a long voyage from Europe to Australia, where weeks were spent without touching land.

Our reader's chum said that following a routine was the best way forward, though he added that he was now at risk of turning his living room into the Officers' Bar.

CONFUSED Nina Buckley asks: "Why is it called 'Road-map out of Lockdown' and not 'Road to De-Mask-Us?'"

2
Let the Earthquake Commence!

KNOWING the huge influence the Diary has on the hearts and minds of the nation, we have until now resisted revealing who we favour when it comes to politics. For the sake of fair-mindedness and balance, this seemed like the ethically sound course of action to follow. However, we are currently living through a revolutionary era. So to heck with our former scruples. At long last we are willing to reveal our preferences . . .

We believe that none of the preening popinjays currently strutting the public stage cut the mustard. In truth, they consistently fail to slice through any condiment you care to mention.

They are all just so (shudder) sincere. Where are the wacky, way-out politicians like Tuxedo Stan, the cat who once stood for office in Nova Scotia?

Or Tião, the grumpy chimpanzee, who bravely attempted to get elected in Rio de Janeiro?

If our politicians resolutely refuse to be outwardly daffy, ditzy or dunderheedish, then clearly it's up to the Diary to scrabble about in the dirt unearthing their most embarrassing moments . . .

IT has been revealed that Boris Johnson – our nation's supremely focused leader, who always has a keen eye for detail – has been ambling around not realising his mobile phone number was freely available online for years.

The PM has at last changed the digits for something more private.

Sadly, this means that the sixty-eight million residents of the UK can no longer give Boris a bell at three in the morning to discuss Brexit, Covid, poor choices in hairdressing salons . . . or any other subject of global importance that comes to mind.

Martin Morrison from Lochinver believes there might have been a more satisfying solution to Johnson's difficulties.

"A lot of problems could be solved if, instead of changing his phone number, he changed his address," he suggests.

BORIS Johnson and fiancée Carrie Symonds were reported to be organising a lavish wedding for themselves. Reader Alex McDougall was curious to know who would fund the shindig, and suggested some possibilities.

1) The British taxpayer.
2) Wealthy Tory donors.
3) Boris will hire an underling to ghostwrite a money-spinning sequel to his book about Shakespeare.
4) Our generous leader will pay for the bash out of his own Prime Ministerial wages.

P.S. We happen to believe one of these suggestions is a non-starter. Can you possibly guess which?

MORE speculation about the Prime Minister's wedding. Reader Fiona Sutherland says: "I'm sure the nuptials will go swimmingly, as long as Dominic Cummings doesn't pop up unexpectedly to give a surprise Best Man's Speech."

THE animosity between Nicola Sturgeon and Alex Salmond continues to snap, crackle and pop, like a particularly obstreperous breakfast cereal. Confused English journalists are desperately trying to get up to speed with our nation's pugnacious and puzzling brand of politics.

On Twitter, former *Guardian* columnist Suzanne Moore sounds like an errant schoolgirl who has forgotten to do her homework, and hopes a chum will help out, when she writes: "What IS happening in Scotland? In one tweet please."

CERTAIN words have been banned from use in Scrabble. The reason being that they don't meet the demanding diktats of those woke apparatchiks who now control vast swathes of modern life and language.

Boardgame fan John Fallon is exasperated by this development. "What next?" he groans. "Perhaps Nicola Sturgeon will ban every letter used in Scrabble, apart from the letters S, N and P."

FORMER Glasgow Labour MP Tom Harris is occasionally recognised by his erstwhile constituents while walking the dog.

With no future ambitions to run for Parliament, Tom no longer feels any compunction to smile politely and tolerate temper tantrums from those he once served.

For example, a complete stranger recently identified him, then pointed to a pothole in the road before demanding that Tom do something about it.

The fellow proceeded to lecture his former parliamentarian about how all politicians are crooks and liars.

Tom waited for the chippy chappy to finish his harangue then languidly informed him that he was: "Talking out of his a**e."

An observation Tom found it most liberating to share with the fellow.

HAVING diligently studied the current political scene, an observant Wishaw reader concludes that Boris Johnson's splendid hairstyle is not the result of visiting a swish and swanky salon.

Instead, our correspondent believes BoJo's fiendishly foppish "Loopy Lear Lurking on the Heath" coiffure was created when the PM jammed his fingers into a live electrical socket.

The Diary feels duty-bound to add that such behaviour should not be practised at home.

(By which we mean jamming one's fingers in a live electrical socket.

Or becoming Prime Minister.

Either activity is seriously bad for one's health.)

OUR readers have been questioning the hirsuteability of a certain B. Johnson of Number Ten Downing Street to lead a great nation.

David Miller of Milngavie recalls it being said of union firebrand Arthur Scargill that he was a three-Shredded-Wheat-a-day man, and believes the same is true of our magnificent Prime Minister.

For, like Scargill of yore, he appears to eat two and plonk one on his head.

ANOTHER tale of the rascally behaviour of former Labour MP, Tom Harris.

Tom had just picked up his sons from school and was driving them to Greggs for a wee snack. Returning with the baked goods, he was astonished to discover he was locked out of his car.

Naturally he tried valiantly to tug open the door, before realising his car was parked behind the one he was in the process of breaking into.

Tom, of course, was mortified.

And his sons?

Devilishly delighted by their father's near fatal faux pas.

IN a bitter and fractious political year there was a point when it was seriously debated whether the Prime Minister should be allowed to visit a certain northern part of the United Kingdom. (It was Scotland, in case you haven't guessed.)

Reader Christine Brooks argues that Boris will always receive a warm welcome in . . . Toryglen.

WATCHING the TV news can be a dispiriting affair, points out David Kirkwood. Though not always for the obvious reasons. "What is it with BBC Scotland that they cannot have enough presenters named Laura?" harrumphs our reader, before proceeding to list such notable anchor women as Laura Maxwell, Laura Miller, Laura Maciver and Laura Goodwin.

Pausing for only the shortest of breaths, he proceeds to name Laura Bicker and Laura Kuenssberg, too.

With a coda of optimism to round off his diatribe, David says: "One day I look forward to watching the news being reported by someone called Senga."

MUSICAL combo The Proclaimers have come out in support of Alex Salmond's Alba Party, which strikes reader Nick Pattison as a tad unfair. "Craig and Charlie Reid have always been ardent nationalists," points out Nick. "But being twins, couldn't they have spread the tartan love around a bit, with one supporting the SNP and the other going for Alba?"

AND talking of Scotland's newest bagpipe and gripe party . . . Michael Dickinson from Falkirk cynically claims the Alba Party won't further the cause of independence, but will instead stymie it. Our reader adds: "I bet Nicola Sturgeon calls it the Alba-tross Round My Neck Party."

CONCERNED reader James Wade is growing increasingly nervous that Alex Salmond's Alba Party will gain prominence in public life. "I'm starting to conceive of a terrifying coalition between Alba and the Scottish Greens," hisses our reader conspiratorially. He adds: "It would, of course, inevitably become known as the Alex Harvie Band."

(Alas, the Greens and SNP teamed up instead. Proving that of all the many faults of our political parties, the greatest is that they wilfully ignore an amusing pun when it's clearly up for grabs.)

THE achievements of British prime ministers are often celebrated at a great distance from their native shores. Gordon Casely was once cycling in New Zealand when he came across a Thatcher Street in the nation's capital of Wellington. Our reader adds: "The bad news was that Thatcher Street bore a sign which read: 'No Exit'."

Which is a neat summation of life in Thatcher's Britain, some would argue.

RETIRED MP Sir Brian Donohoe recalls an occasion when the former Deputy Prime Minister Geoffrey Howe was campaigning in Irvine during a general election and introduced himself to an old lady.

"Hello. I'm Geoffrey Howe," said he.

"Who?" said she.

"No, it's Howe," persisted the politico.

OUR politics increasingly has a sepia-tinted, retro vibe. Alex Salmond on the scene again. George Galloway's fedora hat bobbing into view.

Even an ancient King of Scotland has returned to have his say, courtesy of Hollywood actor and serial Robert the Bruce impersonator, Angus Macfadyen, who is once again performing as the Bruce in a voice-over for an Alba Party video.

Not all of Angus's fellow thespians are impressed. *River City* star David Paisley says: "I know the Alba Party is seen as regressive. But I wasn't expecting to be dragged back to the 1300s."

POLITICAL campaigning can be surreal. Iain Macdonald from Oban questions the decision-making prowess of Scottish Conservative leader Douglas Ross, who allowed himself to be photographed staring contemplatively at a brick.

"What will the nationalists think?" enquires our reader.

More to the point, the Diary demands to know if the brick consented to be photographed with Mr Ross.

It may very well be a nationalist brick, after all. (Though we hear rumours that grouting invariably votes Green.)

AUTHOR Deedee Cuddihy was strolling round Bingham's Pond near Gartnavel Hospital when she overheard a group of women having a blether. The conversation turned to politics and the forthcoming local election. Said one of the group, referring to Nicola Sturgeon: "She says: 'Vote for us and we'll do this and we'll do that . . .'"

To which another member of the group chimed in: "And I say: 'Dae it – and THEN we'll vote fer youse!'"

WE continue to focus on political campaigning in Scotia. James Thomson from Jordanhill suspects the Liberal Democrats are struggling for press coverage. His evidence is not the lack of column inches in newspapers, or web links on the net, but the latest Lib Dem flyer that was posted through his letter box.

The flyer gives an anti-SNP quote, from a national daily newspaper. It then gives an anti-Tory quote, from a national daily newspaper. Finally, and triumphantly, it gives a pro-Willie Rennie quote.

And the source of this momentous and historic statement?

Thomas and Angela – Inverness.

OCCASIONALLY the Diary attempts to burrow inside the head of our glorious leader, who is also an avid reader, by checking out the literature on Nicola Sturgeon's nightstand.

We hear she recently purchased a copy of Edith Wharton's novel *The Gods Arrive*. With a title like that, perhaps Nicola assumes the book is about the momentous occasion when the mighty SNP first exploded on the scene.

Though a more cynical scholar of recent events might conclude that if the book was indeed about the SNP, its title would be: *The Squabbling, Back-Biting and Tearing Themselves Apart Mere Mortals Arrive*.

COMEDIAN Fred MacAulay has been immersing himself in the televised political debates that have showcased the talents of our magnificent Holyrood representatives, and he's ever so impressed.

"Regretting the cancellation of my BT Sport account," he grunts.

WATCHING the TV news, Bill Hutcheson from Paisley was intrigued when the subtitles claimed Anas Sarwar was campaigning in Merry Hell.

This report was confusing for two reasons. First, it suggested that the chaps running Hell might be slacking off when it comes to pitchforking the local population.

Second, it implied that Hell is a Scottish constituency, winnable by Labour in the forthcoming local election.

It transpired that the subtitles should have read Maryhill, not Merry Hell. Though it remains to be seen if that particular location is more winnable for Labour than Hades.

WE mentioned that our glorious leader Nicola Sturgeon is an avid reader of novels. Russell Smith from Largs wonders what fiction her rival commander-in-chief from the Alba Party peruses.

Witnessing Mr Salmond's ebullient swagger and preening self-confidence on the campaign trail, he suggests . . . *Alex in Wonderland.*

SO what books should fiction fan Nicola Sturgeon be reading? A Diary correspondent suggests she should peruse *Salmond Fishing in the Yemen.*

Once she's finished with that she should try *La Peste.* "It's an account by Albert Camus of the plague," he explains, "not about a particularly annoying rival."

WHILE electioneering for seats in the Scottish Parliament, Alex Salmond was his usual demure and understated self. In one especially humble statement about his new party's impact, he roared: "Let the earthquake commence!"

Reader Colin Sullivan says: "If this latest political man-oeuvre doesn't work out for Alex, he can surely get a job writing dialogue for superhero movies."

THE techy gurus who run Silicon Valley banned Donald Trump from Twitter while he was still President, claiming his remarks on the social media site were incendiary.

Arthur Frame from Lanark says: "Just wondering if I've

got this right. The person who had all of America's nuclear codes was deemed too dangerous to have a Twitter account . . . wow."

(When Arthur says "wow" we assume he means "yikes".)

JUST when we thought America couldn't plunge any further into chaos and darkness, a Washington wipeout takes place.

Events move rapidly from chaotic to Krakatoa-ic as the White House is stormed by a ragtag rabble of vagabond varmints. Donald Trump, who was in the process of grudgingly vacating the White House at the time, was accused of supporting the insurrectionists.

Glasgow comedian and close observer of all things American, Paul McDaniel, found the situation most illuminating.

"I tell you what," he observantly opined, "the more I read about this Donald Trump fella, the less I like him."

AN East Dunbartonshire resident rushes to the defence of The Donald, claiming that his critics are being unfair. He argues that Trump's Teutonic background (his dad was of German stock) surely explains at least one foolish remark he made.

For when Trump claimed the election was "stolen, for Biden" he meant to say it was "stollen for Biden".

In other words, winning was a piece of cake for Joe.

IN 2021 the world finally got to say: "Ta-ta, Trump!" And many courageous folk concluded that they could just about survive without him.

Though reader James Harris was distraught, whimpering: "Does this mean it's too late for Donald to pardon Neil Lennon?"

ONE of the difficulties faced by Scotland's football team at the Euros was a lack of goals. Only one shot hit the back of the net in three games.

Reader Bob Davies says: "We need to find someone who doesn't have any problems scoring. I wonder if the SFA have checked if Matt Hancock has Scottish ancestry?"

(By the way, that's the only joke we'll be making about poor Mr Hancock in this chapter. True, he refused to follow the rules he dictated to the rest of the country during lockdown.

Though eventually his error of judgement was discovered and he paid for his mistake with his job. So let's not kick a chap when he's down.)

ALEX Salmond's Alba Party has social media frothing as though an Alka-Seltzer had been crushed into the laptops of a hundred thousand keyboard warriors. One point of contention is whether Salmond is pronouncing the name of his own political organisation correctly. (It's the "Alba" part people dispute. Experts are in agreement that he manages to utter the word "Party" like a true pro.)

Clearly a linguistic minefield lies ahead for this new iteration of Scottish nationalism.

The Diary recommends that for his own safety Mr Salmond should in future steer clear of mentioning Sauchiehall Street, Ecclefechan or Keppochhill Road.

SKY Sports broadcaster Anthony Joseph recently became a dad. The baby is called Alba Grace.

"Nice to hear they've named a party in Scotland after my daughter," says Anthony.

A HARTLEPOOL by-election result emphasises the disconnect between the local working class and the Labour Party, notes former Falkirk MP Dennis Canavan. It also reminds him of the time Peter Mandelson was selected as Hartlepool candidate. He was said to have wandered into a local chip shop where the favourite delicacy was chips and mushy peas.

When asked by a customer what he thought of the food, Mandelson replied: "The chips were quite good but the guacamole was squisita."

THE Holyrood election was the inspiration for numerous astute observations from celebrated commentators, though none of the analysis on offer was as profound as that provided by the Diary.

For example, Bert Peattie from Kirkcaldy noted that Alba failed to gain a single Holyrood seat, despite winning the Eurovision Song Contest (albeit back in the 1970s) and having a smash-hit musical on both sides of the Atlantic.

On further consideration, Bert might want to swap one of those letters in Alba before developing his thesis any further . . .

THE Prime Minister promised to promote environmental policies at the 2021 G7 conference in Cornwall. Reader Dan Percy pinpoints a certain irony: "Boris talks up his green agenda while roaring down to the South West of England in a private jet. He couldn't be less green if he lopped the top off Ben Nevis and replaced it with a Victorian chimney stack."

CONTINUING with the above theme, reader Nigel Clarke points out: "G7 sounds like Boris Johnson guessing how many kids he's got."

THE Diary likes to provide a glimpse behind the dazzling facade that is cunningly constructed by politicians and their acolytes.

For example, we exclusively revealed at the beginning of this chapter that Boris Johnson isn't a particularly disciplined, sombre or hard-working chap. No doubt this revelation came as a shock to readers who believed BoJo was a blend of Churchill, Lincoln and William Wallace.

Russell Smith from Largs points out that all politicians are flawed, even mighty Maggie Thatcher, who once commended her loyal sidekick William Whitelaw by claiming: "Every Prime Minister needs a Willie."

She could easily have retracted this indecorous statement.

But, alas, the lady was not for turning.

WITH an ear to the ground in Westminster, reader Lindsay Young tells us of an unsubstantiated rumour that Matt Hancock wasn't actually caught kissing his colleague, as was previously believed. He was merely using his tongue to explain where to swab for a Covid test.

(Okay, that was a wee bit sneaky. We promised to leave Mr Hancock alone for the remainder of this chapter. Though it seems we don't always practise what we preach. Now who does *that* remind us of?)

RUTH Davidson was formally introduced in the House of Lords, where she is now addressed rather splendiferously as

Baroness Davidson of Lundin Links. Her title is a nod to the Fife coastal town where she was raised.

A reader suggests that the former Scottish Conservative Party leader isn't quite as focused on her home nation as once she was.

"Surely Ruth's House of Lords title contains a spelling mistake," claims our reader. "It should actually be Baroness Davidson of London Links."

PUGNACIOUS political pontificator Nigel Farage joins GB News, the broadcasting station launched by Paisley's very own Andrew Neil who later resigned . . .

Farage, who is anchoring a current affairs show, is a rather divisive chap. If you could pour a family-sized jar of Marmite into an empty double-breasted suit it would probably have some sort of resemblance to Nigel.

Andrew Adonis, the splendidly named Blairite politico, is certainly no fan of either Farage or the high heed yin of GB News.

On social media Adonis harrumphs: "So, as many of us always argued, Andrew Neil was John the Baptist to Farage."

This surely is thrilling news for biblical scholars. Who could have guessed that John the Baptist was a Paisley buddy?

A RADIO TIMES poll has voted Sean Connery the greatest-ever James Bond. With this in mind, we've devised a cunning plan to maintain the movie franchise's appeal once Daniel Craig quits, by replacing the ageing *Bond* star with another Son of Alba.

One possibility is Scottish Tory leader, and qualified football referee, Douglas Ross. Here's a scene from our proposed flick. Ross meets spy boss M . . .

M: Are you a patriot, Mr Ross?

Ross: Yes, sir! Union Jack undies. Maggie Thatcher lunch box. British Bulldog soft toy for nighty-night cuddles . . .

M: Handle a weapon?

Ross: I can stop a man in his tracks with . . . this!

(*Ross pulls a Red Card from his pocket.*)

M: Not good enough, I'm afraid. Next candidate! Now you look REALLY promising. So, Ms Davidson. Or may I call you Ruth . . .?

THERE'S been quite a gap since we last broke our pledge and published another snide comment about Matt Hancock – the last one was at least three whole stories ago.

We've decided to celebrate our commendable show of restraint . . . by publishing another snide comment about Matt Hancock.

Still Game and *River City* star Sanjeev Kohli says: "They've put together an edited package of all of Matt Hancock's gaffes, and it's longer than his actual career."

3

The Fame Game

A FAMOUS chap celebrated his sixtieth birthday this past year. A fellow in fine fettle who has avoided all of time's spiteful depredations.

His body remains trim. There is no loss of hair. And when it comes to clothes, he ain't no fashion victim . . . he's a fashion victor, baby.

So let's hear it for Ken, Barbie's boyfriend.

Though perhaps the ultimate toy boy is just a little bit too perfect. Those frozen features. That plastic grin.

Then there's the persistent rumours. The Diary's showbiz contacts whisper about an alleged nip and tuck. And is the Barbie/Ken romance built on solid foundations? Or do the cunning couple stay together in the hope of bagging their very own Kardashian-style reality TV show?

It's all so confusing. The truth is you just never know where you are with those slippery celebs, as you'll soon discover . . .

YOUR average debauched rock god used to spend his days chucking TV sets out of hotel windows.

The destructive activities of Justin Currie, lead singer with Glasgow band Del Amitri, are slightly more commonplace. He dropped eggs on the floor while preparing breakfast.

Apparently, the incident was the result of a hefty static shock from the cooker, which bent Justin's favourite frying pan and left him screaming.

Alas, the fallen eggs couldn't be saved, though Justin thought about applying the 'five second rule' allowing him to pluck the shattered remnants of his meal from the floor before gobbling up all that yolky goodness.

Though he quickly changed his mind.

"I've not mopped that floor since 2007," he explained.

A STORM cloud drifts over the usually immaculate presentational skills of BBC weather woman Carol Kirkwood. During a breakfast forecast, live from London's Greenwich Park, she describes the scene with lilting enthusiasm: "Fabulous! The sun is beating down. We've seen lots of doggers."

She possibly means dog walkers. Though that London Town is known for its eclectic and energetic social life . . .

THE wife of *Outlander* actor Steven Cree was on a Zoom call. "I had no idea," explains Steven, "and walked by in the background, completely naked, fresh out of the shower."

Steven should look on the bright side. Most actors are

desperately looking for that special role that reveals their — ahem — hidden talents.

THE Diary was intrigued to learn that the movie star Michael Madsen was visiting Edinburgh's Royal Highland Centre in October, as a guest at Comic Con Scotland.

Madsen has appeared in numerous films, including Quentin Tarantino classics *Reservoir Dogs*, *Kill Bill* and *The Hateful Eight*.

He specialises in playing crazed, violent chaps who like to snarl and rip and crush and gouge. (Not necessarily in that order.) Less well known is his sensitive side. Madsen's a published poet.

So, does the gentle soul write about daffodils and sunsets? Well, here's a clue. Poetry books that he's published have titles such as *Beer, Blood and Ashes*, *Eat the Worm* and *When Pets Kill*.

Hmmm.

Perhaps we overstated Madsen's sensitive side, just a tad.

SCOTTISH actor and sports fan Douglas Henshall admits he doesn't understand American football, even though he has been watching it since 1984.

After conducting some research, the Diary concludes it's actually a rather simple activity.

American football is just British football, blended with the Battle of Stalingrad.

(With a few motorcycle helmets tossed onto the field of combat to keep the casualties as low as possible.)

SCOTTISH playwright Daniel Jackson (known as D.C. Jackson to theatrical types) finds himself in an exasperated mood. "My baby son is so noisy it's like having a goose," he says.

Barely able to suppress a sigh of discontent at the many disappointments even a proud parent must endure, he adds: "Of course, with a goose you'd get eggs."

ACTOR Jordan Young, of *River City* fame, had a dream that he was in a play with Robert De Niro. "He stabbed me for real because he didn't like me, or rate me," sighs Jordan. On a more positive note, he adds: "It was still an honour to share a stage with him."

THE approach of Valentine's Day led to a tender, romantic moment for Bathgate comedian Fern Brady, whose boyfriend said to her: "I suppose I'd marry you as a practical recognition of our financial bond together."

A completely smitten Fern swooned: "OMG, he's the sweetest!"

GLASGOW crime writer Douglas Skelton has been investigating commercials. "All these detergent ads now end with the warning to always keep away from children," he says, before adding proudly: "Been staying away from them for years."

BBC Middle East Correspondent Martin Patience, who originally hails from Scotland, admits to being a very proud daddy when he spotted his young son sitting diligently reading a comic book for an hour.

"Turns out it was hiding an iPad," sighs Martin. "Good effort though."

(And, no, the iPad wasn't logged into an online version of *War and Peace*. The little chap was playing computer games.)

CONFUSED chanteuse Amy Macdonald is intrigued by a new drama on ITV called *Finding Alice*, though there also happens to be another drama on Apple TV called *Losing Alice*.

"I think I need to know more about Alice before I choose which one to watch," concedes the sensibly cautious pop star.

MORE on the misgivings of songstress Amy Mac. Alastair J. Douglas from Erskine commiserates with the pop star and her angsty Alice dilemma. He suggests that Amy should undertake some intrepid detective work by getting in touch with 1970s pop band, Smokie, who were, of course, last heard of Living Next Door to Alice.

SCOTTISH golf broadcaster Diane Knox is based in the States, though her connections to Scotia remain robust. She even owns a framed picture of a certain statue of the Duke of Wellington wearing a traffic cone hat.

Recently her boyfriend surprised her with a gift he bought to remind Diane of her native land. An ornamental glass cow. At first glance it doesn't seem particularly Scottish, though Diane explains it harks back to home because: "When I talk to Americans about Glasgow, they pronounce it Glass-Cow."

THE main reason for the Diary's existence is to provide succour for those in most need. In this chapter this has largely meant helping singer Amy Macdonald, who as we've seen, is swithering over whether to watch new TV programme *Finding Alice*, or the similarly sounding show *Losing Alice*.

As Amy previously pointed out, she really needs to know more about this mysterious female before bracing herself for the shock of either gaining or being deprived of her.

Reader George Kelly suggests that Macdonald should get in touch with fellow musician Arlo Guthrie, who apparently has been claiming that Alice joined the service industry in some sort of managerial capacity . . .

EDINBURGH crime scribe Ian Rankin uses his highly developed puzzling abilities to complete jigsaws. Which sounds rather impressive. Though further investigation reveals he's been working on a Beatles jigsaw, though only of Paul McCartney's face.

Which is about as impressive as completing a Lulu jigsaw which only includes one Lu.

SMOOTH-talking radio broadcaster Ken Bruce and his producer Phil McGarvey devised the perfect title for the next album from Scottish pop sensation Lewis Capaldi. They suggest *Giving It Laldy* by Lewis Capaldi. (With a possible commercial tie-in with Aldi . . .)

SPY novelist John le Carré was an ethical sort of chap whose commitment to fairness and justice once helped a certain Scottish movie icon bag a plum role.

When the film was being made of le Carré's *The Russia House* the plan was to have Jeremy Irons in the lead, though an epic battle in a London park put paid to that.

"Irons's vicious dogs attacked my smaller dogs," fumed le Carré at the time. "He never stooped to apologise."

The movie role instead went to Sean Connery.

Sometimes it pays not to have a dog in the fight.

WHEN you are a windswept and interesting broadcaster such as Neil Oliver, mail tends to reach you, even when the sender isn't entirely sure of your precise location.

The postman recently brought Neil a letter addressed to:

Scottish Bloke With Long Hair,
Hangs Around Coastal Regions,
Stirling,
Scotland.

PAISLEY reader Mary Christie is curious to know if other celebrities also receive letters with a vague address on the envelope. To discover if they do, she intends mailing a missive to:

Mr & Mrs Moany-Whiny-Greetin' Faces
Vast Wealth Avenue,
(Opposite Easy Street)
Sunny California.

Mary refuses to reveal who the intended recipients of her letter happen to be, though she does supply us with two subtle clues.

1) They just might be members of the Royal Family.

2) Their names just might rhyme with Barry and Fleghan.

IT possibly isn't only Neil Oliver who receives mystery mail. Ian Noble from Carstairs Village informs us of an apocryphal tale involving a Royal Mail team tasked with solving cryptic addresses. One envelope was addressed to:

Wood

John

Hants

It was correctly deciphered as:

John Underwood

Andover

Hants

MYSTERY mail continued . . . We are told of a woman who always wrote in an illegible scrawl.

She once addressed a birthday card to her sister in Leven, Fife.

And it duly arrived. Several months later.

(Having first been delivered to Viti Levu, Fiji.)

ERIC Simmons from Edinburgh used to practise as a solicitor in Dunbar and once received a letter addressed to "The Lawyer, Dunbar".

"As there were two other legal firms in the town, I took that as a compliment," chuckles Eric.

UNLIKE all those letters addressed to Neil Oliver, we seem to have veered off track a tad. After all, this chapter is meant to be about sassy celeb shenanigans.

So back to those fame-frazzled folk we go . . .

STIRLING-based novelist Ross Sayers is feeling accomplished. "Just wrote 'The End' on my latest book!" he exclaims.

With slightly less enthusiasm he adds: "I think it's a really strong opening sentence and I can't wait to write more."

DOUGLAS Stuart won the Booker Prize for his gritty Glasgow novel *Shuggie Bain*, though he long ago flitted from Scotland to the high-wattage dazzle of New York.

Still, Douglas admits that the Big Apple's high watt sometimes turns into more of a: "Hey! What?!"

For example, he recently ordered a sandwich in a New York deli. "They ladled HOT ketchup all over it," he shudders. "Like ketchup they warmed in an urn. It made the whole thing taste like it had been pre-chewed by someone else."

No doubt dreaming of the more dignified splendours of a poke of chips, Douglas concludes haughtily: "Not cool, NYC."

AFTER the sad death of Prince Philip, political parties agreed to temporarily stop campaigning out of a mark of respect.

Leith-based comedian Jo Caulfield noted: "They will continue their disrespectful behaviour next week."

WHEN Pure Radio Scotland presenter Amber Zoe was six she drew a picture to celebrate her mother's birthday. The colourful scrawl showed Amber's mum being pummelled in the face.

And the reason Amber concocted such a worryingly violent image?

"I thought a 'birthday bash' was a square go," she admits.

ELFIN-faced thespian David Tennant celebrates a milestone birthday. (Shhh. Don't tell anyone. It's the big five uh-oh.) On social media his enthusiastic legion of fans celebrates with him, recalling his best moments on screen.

One acolyte holds a rather eccentric view of his hero's acting career, toasting Tennant's titanic talents by writing: "Happy 50th birthday David Tennant. Yes, yes, *Doctor Who, Broadchurch,* blah blah blah. Everyone knows your best role was Sir Piers Pomfrey in *St Trinians 2: The Legend of Fritton's Gold.*"

And just in case you're feeling culturally clueless.

Nope.

We haven't heard of it, either.

BBC crime drama *Line of Duty* is getting fans all hot and bothered with its numerous twists and turns. Though not every viewer is intrigued by the plot. Ignoring the more obvious dramatic developments on screen, broadcaster Muriel Gray notes the acronym GSW is used in the show to mean Gun Shot Wounds. But, as she points out, the abbreviation has more syllables than the actual words, meaning it takes longer to say.

"Should I write to the police?" she wonders. "Might they find it useful? I might get a certificate or a badge or something."

GRAEME Armstrong's novel about gang culture in Airdrie, *The Young Team*, which is based on his frisky and fractious youth, is being adapted for television.

With a poetic flourish, Graeme describes his transformation from marginalised man to Mr Media Mogul:

"Fae roaming the schemes,

Tae yer TV screens . . ."

AT eighty-two years old, Sir Ian McKellen became the oldest professional thespian to play Hamlet. Writer Ian Pattison (the chap who brought you *Rab C. Nesbitt*) met McKellen many times when both men lived in London, always in Kensington. Their conversations were invariably cordial, succinct and professional, and usually went like this:

McKellen: A bottle of Gordon's Gin please, and six Schweppes tonics.

Pattison: Certainly.

McKellen: Could you put it on my account, please?

Pattison: Certainly.

McKellen: Thank you. Goodbye.

Pattison: Thank you. Goodbye.

Pattison tells the Diary: "I once made the mistake of asking him if he'd like a bag. He answered in blank verse. It took a long time. I looked like Yorick by the time he'd finished."

(Most of the above is true, we should add. Though as the vignette makes clear, when these conversations took place, Ian Pattison hadn't quite completed the aspiring bit of the aspiring writer gig.)

EDINBURGH comedian Martin Bearne emailed a poem to his therapist but she couldn't open the file. "Not the first time we've had attachment issues," sighs Martin.

NOVELIST Douglas Stuart woke early to do a radio interview, but became distracted as he only had one shoe on because he couldn't find its partner.

This wasn't his first footy faux pas: "I've gone to the pub in my slippers before," he sighs.

SCIENTISTS haven't managed to rocket humans to Mars yet. Though they have come up with PawSense, a computer programme that detects when your cat is walking on your keyboard. It then blocks typing and plays a sound to scare it away.

Fife comedian Richard Pulsford is most impressed by this blocking ability.

"It puts everything on paws?" he marvels.

AS we previously mentioned, *Line of Duty*, starring Greenock thespian Martin Compston, has been the smash hit of the TV year. National Museums Scotland were most impressed with Martin's performance and admit that they would like to display one of the iconic waistcoats he wore with such aplomb on the show.

And here was the Diary assuming that museums could only display ancient artifacts such as brontosaurus bones, rusty broadswords . . . and the school blazer worn by wee Jimmy Krankie.

WRITER and producer Mark Millar is one of the most in-demand hotshots in Hollywood, constantly developing high profile films and TV shows.

Jupiter's Legacy, his latest series, was launched on Netflix with much fanfare. And the Coatbridge-raised mover and shaker celebrated in style, like a true movie mogul . . . by enjoying a day in Ayr with his family.

The weather was freezing and the kids complained piteously while icy rain hammered their faces as they shuddered on the beach.

"But they'll look back on all this with fond memories," claims Mark, who also enjoyed a deep-fried pizza and chips at a local café.

ACTOR, comedian and former Glasgow resident Johnny Vegas reveals that he tackled his own stunts in TV show *Murder, They Hope*. As did fellow star Sian Gibson.

Though Johnny accepts his limitations. "Sian's always coming up with things for me to do," he explains. "Being the committed actor I am, I always say, 'I think my character would walk off screen . . .' just to get back to my trailer."

WE have mentioned that National Museums Scotland want to exhibit one of the natty waistcoats worn by actor Martin Compston.

Reader Ralph Bennett wonders what other fine Scottish artifacts could be displayed. "Perhaps that boulder with a quote from Alex Salmond, which used to sit in the grounds of Heriot-Watt Uni," he muses. "It could be displayed in an exhibition about political bombast gone bust."

DO we live in a world of safety-swaddling, mollycoddling mums and dads, wonders Perth comedian Joe Heenan. "I gave my ten-year-old son a big row for not wearing his helmet when he was out riding his bike," says Joe. "Then I remembered when I was his age I would spend all day with my mates playing in a disused, crumbling asbestos factory."

MONTY Python star Eric Idle reveals he once took part in what must be the most daffily diverse music session of all time.

After a Billy Connolly performance at the Hammersmith Odeon, Eric jammed with the Big Yin himself, along with late Paisley rocker Gerry Rafferty and . . . Salman Rushdie.

We wonder what Connolly and Rushdie chatted about after the session. Perhaps Billy complained about the hecklers he's had to deal with in his career, with Rushdie conceding that he's received the occasional minor criticism, too . . .

MARYHILL singer Donovan was part of the psychedelic slew of musicians who made the 60s such a hippy, trippy, deeply dippy decade.

So it's perhaps unsurprising that he recently teamed up with surrealist movie maker David Lynch, who directed the pop star's latest music video.

But is Lynch too wacky even for Donovan? This is the chap, after all, who is rumoured to keep a dead rat in his fridge for inspiration.

The Diary, meanwhile, believes that margarine in the fridge is much more stimulating for the creative juices.

And, unlike a deceased rodent, it has the added benefit that you can spread it on toast.

A FAMOUS musician was staying at a swanky Glasgow hotel. The chef sent a young porter to the star's room to ask what he wanted for dinner, and also to give the porter a chance to meet a celeb.

He knocked on the door and when it opened the star said: "Hi. I'm Hank Marvin."

The porter replied: "The kitchen disnae open till six."

BOB Dylan was once awarded an honorary degree by the University of St Andrews, though the frazzle-haired folk singer left rather hastily after the ceremony. One of the organisers, spotting him rushing off, said to another dignitary, "Quick! Catch him. He's not supposed to take the gown with him."

He received the reply, "If you think I'm going to go running after the spokesman for a generation demanding he return a gown – go yourself."

The gown was never seen again.

THE Diary is admired for many reasons. Our hard-hitting investigative journalism. Our serious and sober tone. And, most importantly, our exclusive celebrity stories. For instance, we were the first to report that *Still Game* star Ford Kiernan was having a rough time back in May.

"Pickled or spring onion crisp breakfast dilemma," he was heard to groan despondently.

AS we pointed out, broadcaster Neil Oliver gets oodles of fan mail. Though he isn't adored by everyone, and his decision to join the freshly launched news channel GB News wasn't universally popular.

Glasgow comedy actor Robert Florence certainly wasn't impressed, claiming Oliver's career had gone from "Coast to toast."

IT'S been a tragic time for pun-loving Fife comedian Richard Pulsford, who sobs: "I've been having a coffee mourning. My espresso machine died."

YOUR average novelist has many enemies. For a start, there's the general public, who all too often refuse to bow down or swoon when confronted with a writer's dazzling genius. Bookshops, too, can be problematic. They've been known to stock works by – yeuch – rival scribblers.

Perhaps the deadliest foe an author faces is their own editor.

Inverness-based crime scribe Shona MacLean, who publishes as S.G. MacLean, once had a copy editor who attempted to replace the word 'cawing' with 'mewing' in reference to an Aberdonian seagull.

"I explained that your average Aberdonian seagull is approximately the size of a small bus," says MacLean, "and it does not mew."

ON social media, the London-based actress Tori Allen-Martin admits she's been suffering. "I have a hangover the size of a tsunami. When will I ever learn?" she groans, adding: "I am a proud Glaswegian until I'm in Glasgow, and then I must remember that I have been watered down by London."

CRIME novelist Liam McIlvanney is the son of that other fine Scottish writer, the late William McIlvanney, who authored many memorable books, including *Laidlaw*.

Stories written by McIlvanney Snr were often gritty and violent. But did such activities overlap into his real life?

It certainly seemed to be the case when Liam, as a young boy, discovered numerous instruction books scattered round the house, all stamped with the letters IRA.

The suspicious volumes turned out to be textbooks from the school where William was at the time teaching English.

Which happened to be Irvine Royal Academy . . . or IRA, for short.

BUSINESSWOMAN Michelle Mone married billionaire Doug Barrowman on the Isle of Man. The lavish celebration included oysters, roast beef and dogs wearing tuxedos.

"Michelle remains a humble Glesga gal at heart," says reader Alexander Blackwood approvingly. "If she'd really wanted to be outrageously excessive, the dogs would have been conveyed in sedan chairs; and, when petted, would bark out the wittier utterances of Noel Coward."

GLASGOW-born screenwriter Kirstie Swain is in a class-conscious frame of mind. "I'm not saying I'm posh," she says. "But I think my baby's first word was 'Aga'."

4

The Broken Strumpet

AS the singer Dinah Washington famously pointed out, 'What a Diff'rence a Day Makes'.

The Holyrood government clearly took those words to heart this year when it revealed plans to trial a four-day working week in Scotland.

The Diary isn't sure what will be the outcome of all this extra chillaxing. We fear it could result in armed robbers racing out of banks carrying hefty bags with SWAG written on the side, only to be momentarily delayed by a policeman, politely asking them to keep the ruckus down a tad, as some off-duty cops are trying to enjoy Piña Coladas in a nearby beer garden.

Even worse, passengers in aeroplanes, flying thousands of feet above Scotland, will look through their windows in horror as they glimpse their pilot parachuting from the cockpit while holding a sign that reads: "Apologies for the inconvenience. My extra day off work starts . . . NOW."

Luckily our Diary contributors never take time off. They unceasingly bombard us with crackpot comments and titter-tastic tales, such as the ones you will find in the following chapter . . .

OUR correspondents always look forward to convivial times ahead. They also like to recall affable occasions of old.

Mary Duncan tells us of the famous Glasgow folk singer who arrived at a friend's door bearing a carry-out and was invited in. After a while he asked his host when the others were coming.

"You mean for the party?" enquired the host.

"Yes," agreed the folk singer.

"That was last night," he was informed. "And you were at it."

DECIDING to get spruced up, a Hamilton reader went for a haircut and was confronted by a line of chaps waiting in the street due to limited numbers allowed inside.

A chuckle broke out when, in the glorious sunshine, our reader quipped: "Smashing day for a barber's queue."

THINKING about holidays, reader Sylvia Glover says: "The best thing about camping is when you get sick of it and go to a hotel."

THERE was a business in one of Glasgow's rougher parts run by a father and daughter. The pair regularly visited the office of David Miller from Milngavie, who delighted in the Glesga patter exchanged between them, which continued even after one of them had slipped the mortal coil.

David recalls standing next to the daughter as her father's coffin was lowered into its grave and the heavens opened, drenching them.

The daughter turned to our reader and whispered: "I'll bet the auld b****r arranged this."

THE University of Hull revealed they won't demand correct spelling from the work of their scholars as they claim that would be elitist. Which reminds us of a Chic Murray line: "Just because you can't spell 'Armageddon', it's not the end of the world."

ONE of the university chums of reader Bob Byiers spent a year studying in Germany. One evening the lightbulb went out in his room.

"Apparently there are two words in German which sound and look very similar, but have quite different meanings," says Bob, whose friend rather unfortunately chose the wrong one.

He ended up complaining to his landlord that the strumpet in his room wasn't working.

A DIARY photo of a curious street name inspires Doug Maughan to inform us that the police station at RAF Mount Pleasant in the Falkland Islands is on . . . Letsby Avenue.

ANOTHER peculiar place name. We are informed that in Dundee there is a road called Horsewater Wynd which – coincidentally or not – leads to Smellies Lane.

LECTURING to a rapt audience is a thrilling experience. It can also be humbling. Malcolm Boyd from Milngavie gave an illustrated talk to a history group. The chairman of the organisation mentioned in his welcome address that Malcolm was giving his talk free of charge.

This meant, the chairman added approvingly, that for the group's next meeting they could afford a good speaker.

THERE'S a language barrier that exists between Scotland and everyone else on the planet. The sort of barrier that makes a crocodile-infested moat and castle drawbridge look like a 'Welcome!' doormat. Richard Davis once lived in Austria where he regularly attended hospital to see a neurologist. Doctor and patient usually had no difficulty communicating in English. Though Richard was once lying on the examination couch while the doc asked if he could feel a sharp needle pricking his foot.

Forgetting where he was, Richard replied, "Och, just a wee bit," causing the muddled medic to march to the head of the table to demand an immediate translation.

VACATIONING in France, a reader spotted a cute puppy scampering round a farm. So he took his kids to see it.

The word for puppy in French is *chiot*. Though our reader forgot that you don't pronounce the final t.

As a result he received a most quizzical look from Mme Dumoulin of the farm when he politely enquired if he could see her *chiotte*.

In other words, her outside toilet.

(Actually, the precise English translation of chiotte is slightly more – ahem – robust than outside toilet. Think of the word outhouse, then replace the word 'out' with something that rhymes with twit. Now you're getting the picture.)

THE story above reminds Chas Jessop from Montrose of his student days in France when he played rugby in the nation's lower divisions. Matches often involved visits to small towns in rural areas, referred to as '*la France profonde*'.

If a hapless referee dared to make a decision against the home team the cry would go up from the ever-so-slightly partisan crowd: "*Aux chiottes l'arbitre!*"

"And they weren't referring to puppies," says Chas.

RAMBUNCTIOUS rugby fans – continued. Barrie Crawford played a season in Bavaria where the German supporters were (slightly) more considerate than their Gallic counterparts. The shout of displeasure at a referee's decision was: *"Schiri, ans Telefon!"* i.e., "Ref, you're wanted on the phone!"

ANOTHER linguistic adventure involving Scots abroad. In the 1960s, reader Ally McLaws went on a family holiday to France. Ally's sibling, Marion, was eager to venture out on her own to shop for the daily crusty loaf, so her dad schooled her in the native tongue.

He also advised her that if the shopkeeper asked any follow-up questions, she should respond: *"Je ne dinnae ken pas."*

This she did, though the friendly shopkeeper warmed to her anyway.

THE Scottish Virtual Restaurant Awards took place entirely on the internet. Which led the Diary to ponder if this meant there would also be virtual cash prizes, to be spent on virtual booze, leading to the inevitable virtual morning-after hangover . . .

IT was revealed that UK shops were suffering from a garden gnome shortage. "I'm not in the least upset," shrugged a reader who admitted to despising the jaunty ornaments. "Does that make me gnomophobic?"

MISTAKEN identity. It isn't just a worry for undercover spies. John Mulholland recalls a Sunday many years ago when he and his two-year-old brother were taken by their mum to Mass. The priest walked from the altar to the pulpit. As he climbed the pulpit's spiral staircase he disappeared from view for a split second, only to reappear as if by magic at the top, his arms outstretched in his brightly coloured vestments to announce the reading of the Gospel.

"Oh look, Mummy," shouted John's brother excitedly. "It's a Jack-in-the-box!"

OUR devil-may-care readers report many hair-raising experiences at the hairdressers. Linda Mumphry from Muirend was charged £165 for a basic snippety-snip. Linda knew prices had risen a tad thanks to lockdown, though this seemed a trifle excessive.

"I'm only joking!" chuckled the hairdresser, adding: "But you were going to pay it, weren't you?"

Linda tells us: "I probably would have, too. Though only because I'm seventy-six years old and much too mature to be shoulder-charging past hairdressers and skedaddling out the premises with my purse clasped firmly shut."

STROLLING to the shops with her six-year-old daughter, reader Paula Beasley said: "I could really go a chocolate eclair."

"Who's Clair?" asked the youngster. "And why's she so chocolatey?"

5

The Queen of Lauder's

PAULINE Doyle has been homeless for eighteen months.

Oh sure, she had that place in Edinburgh for a while. But Pauline in Edinburgh was like a salmon sunbathing in the Sahara desert. (Just to clarify, salmon don't enjoy sunbathing in the Sahara desert all that much.)

She also has what you could call her home-home. The place she goes at the end of the night to make dinner, watch TV, fall asleep. That sort of home is in Knightswood.

But the place where Pauline's most alive, most relevant, most adored and most defiantly, unapologetically, triumphantly Pauline?

That all takes place in Lauder's Bar, where she's been a barmaid for almost fifteen years.

No, not just a barmaid. Pauline is the hub, the happening, the her who must be listened to and laughed along with.

So when this venerable old pub was gutted in the infamous fire that tore through parts of Sauchiehall Street in March 2018, Pauline was left bereft . . . and homeless.

"It wis like ma leg had been ripped aff," she tells me, when I pop in to celebrate the pub's relaunch after extensive renovations.

While Lauder's was being brought back to life, its corporate owners, Mitchells & Butlers, sent Pauline to work in one of their Edinburgh bars.

Which felt like banishment for this proud Glesga gal.

Her eyeballs roll at the memory. "That wis an experience," she says. "Funny folk in Embra, God love 'em. Beautiful city and all that. But no banter. I wis goin' aff ma heed."

An elderly fellow dodders into the pub and gazes around, awestruck, like a Victorian Egyptologist cracking open the Great Pyramid of Giza, then savouring the splendours within.

In a shaky voice he says: "Have you been closed, then?"

Pauline snorts: "Where have you been, in a box for the last eighteen months?"

Which may sound a little harsh. But Pauline has the timing of a grouchy, yet lovable, Borscht Belt comedian. Her chat is rat-a-tat rapid. Machine-gun quips that rarely miss their mark.

"Right, eejit, wit you want?" is her welcome for one customer.

To another, she says: "Where you going to sit, pal? And don't say on your backside."

With her banter-chanter bagpiping to one and all, Pauline is one of Lauder's great constants.

She has even created her very own Lauder's gang. Individuals wandered in, one by one. Over time, Pauline forged them into a team of sorts, much like the Avengers, only with pints and paunches rather than muscles and capes.

Pauline has nicknames (or secret identities) for her team of tipplers. "There's George, the resident Old Yin," she says. "He's eighty odds. Got his own special wee tankard. Had to get him a new yin after the fire."

Then there's Tam the Bastard Polis. (Retired member of the local constabulary.) Kenny the Hun. (Rangers fan.) Pauline, herself, is Pauline the Bead Rattler. (Reflecting her Catholic faith.)

All the names are offensive, but nobody takes offence. You'll find no safe spaces in Lauder's.

Since it opened in 1836 it has been a bastion of boisterous behaviour. Located in the centre of Glasgow's theatre land, it was the haunt of music-hall turns and upmarket thespians. Now telly types tipple, too. Plus ordinary punters of every persuasion.

Although slap-bang in the city centre, it has the ambience of a slightly dilapidated village local. Last year's fire, however, instigated radical changes. The decor has been spiffed-up and splendidaffied. Everybody's especially proud of the new toilets. Customers shake their heads in wonderment while talking about them. (Which they do. A lot.)

Overhearing one of these conversations is like listening to a proud parent discussing an errant schoolboy who has now decided to knuckle-down and attend class.

The toilets were once a fetid swamp. A jaded Amazon of exotic aromas and terrible tributaries. The sort of place Indiana Jones might wade through on his way to unearthing another ancient artefact. Alas, no ancient artefact has ever been discovered in the Lauder's toilets. Unless you count auld boozers taking a whiz.

Pauline recalls the toilets of old with a fond, faraway look in her eyes: "We had this guy in the bar who'd been in every jail in Scotland," she says. "He said none of his cells were as bad as our toilets."

Now those very same bogs have been buffed and burnished, as I discover during a forensic examination. (That's right, folks. Some journalists enter the corridors of power to get an exclusive story. I clamber into the cludgie.) Not only are the toilets gleaming, not streaming, but I also spy a jar of hair gel next to the sink. A little something extra for the dapper chapper.

Not that there's an over-representation of dapper chappers in Lauder's.

It's an authentic, old-style Glasgow pub; many of the customers ripped straight out of a black and white photograph, circa 1975.

A wee wummin pops in wi' the shoappin' bags, sneaks a quickie quencher, then is gone. Old boys hunker down by the bar, here until the end of time. Or at least until last orders are called.

There's a smattering of tourists, too, as you would expect in a city-centre boozer, plus the odd trendy. (Very odd indeed, to be a trendy, then rock up at Lauder's.)

Darin McCann is what you would probably call trendy-adjacent. Not quite a hipster. But he does own a man bag, slings it across his shoulder in a raffish manner, and admits to drinking in some of Glasgow's more fashionable watering holes. But he always returns to Lauder's.

"I'm part of the furniture," he says. "I've been coming here fifteen years, which is a long time. Something just draws me back. I'll go into those upmarket bars, but this place brings you down to earth. This is Glasgow. And that's why so many people have been waiting for it to open again."

Darin has worked various jobs, taking him far from Glasgow. But once back in town, he invariably makes a beeline for his favourite drinking den. Like Pauline, he calls Lauder's home. And the men he stands shoulder-to-shoulder with at the bar are family.

Although Darin's a youthful fifty-two, his booze brothers include blokes in their seventies and eighties.

"I used to buy them all their Christmas lunches and drinks," he tells me, with a grin as warm as crackling coal. "They were older gentlemen, living off their pensions, and I had good jobs offshore on boats and rigs. So I was happy to do it."

He adds: "I've lost a lot of older gentlemen over the years.

And I'll be honest with you, it's difficult when you walk back in and they're not here any more."

Darin is so close to his fellow drinkers, and the bar staff, that he can talk to them about anything.

"There are personal things I've only felt I could tell the staff in here," he says. "Things I'm not yet ready to tell my actual family. You stand at the corner of that bar, and you get things off your chest."

He adds: "I like a drink, but it's not really about that. It's about coming in and saying: 'Hi, Pauline. How are you? Hi, George. What're you having?' It's that camaraderie. You look at somebody, and think, that could be my grandfather.

"And see Pauline? She's the glue that holds this pub together. She's not management or anything. But she doesn't have to be. She's still the best-known person in here. The Queen of Lauder's."

Speaking of that eminent royal dignitary . . .

Pauline has just finished her ten-hour shift. But she isn't

leaving. Not yet. Her fella's just arrived, and they'll be having a drink together. Then her mum's coming down.

A family outing, right here, at home. In Lauder's.

Meanwhile, I'm heading towards the front door, out into the Glasgow night. Before I get there, Pauline fires a parting shot in my direction.

"Been oan ma feet all day," she harrumphs. "The oany break I got was talkin' tae you. And that wisnae fun."

So adieu, then, Your Royal Highness. Though before I take my leave, I have to say, the feeling wasn't mutual.

Talking to you, and the rest of the Lauder's gang, was a whole lot of fun.

6

Flicking Spoonfuls

THE Diary was outraged when we heard that production had commenced at Scotland's first commercial gold mine near the village of Tyndrum.

"First commercial gold mine?" we snarled. "First?!"

Everyone knows the Diary has been digging up the shiny yellow stuff for years. From the mindscape of our readers, we chisel anecdotes and quirky comments that are as precious as anything you'll find in a Bank of England vault. These nuggets are then buffed and burnished to perfection before being placed in the ornate display cabinet otherwise known as The Herald Diary Book.

Furthermore, the treasures we unearth continue to increase in value with the passing of time. A story that merely elicits a wry chuckle today will produce a hearty guffaw a few years down the line.

The following tales are among our very best. So no need to visit Tyndrum with a hefty shovel just yet . . .

IN the early hours of the morning a Cairneyhill policeman received a phone call from a hysterical chap, reporting the sighting of an aardvark in his living room.

The anti-aardvark squad duly arrived at the scene, where the homeowner had clearly been imbibing a few liquid refreshments of the non soft-drink variety. The incident was swiftly dealt with by the heroic Boys in Blue, who bravely ejected a rabid brown cushion from the house.

THE friend of a Borders reader was exasperated by badgers who visited his garden nightly. Our reader, who knows the ways of the country, explained to this chap that male human urine is an excellent deterrent, as badgers avoid its scent. The friend thought about this for a while, then he said: "But where would I get male human urine? The Internet, perhaps?"

THE mystery of the century is who is knitting huge fuzzy hats and placing them on top of the postboxes of Greenock? The Diary's top secret Greenock contact, who we imaginatively call Deep Throat, has provided us with visual evidence of three cosily attired postboxes in the district.

We are now puzzling over a couple of pertinent questions:
1) Is this a natural phenomenon, like moss growing on the side of a wall? (Unlikely, as the knitted hats are

decorated with nifty woollen figures, including a snow-man and Santa Claus.)

2) Will this continue until the entire surface of Greenock is coated in wool?

No answers yet, though our investigative team is on the case. The culprit certainly won't pull the wool over our eyes . . .

A FEW years ago, reader Jemima Millard got a job in an office. It seemed that her boss was very impressed with her work, as only a couple of weeks after she joined the firm he said to her: "A large number of new recruits started at the same time as you. But you're the only one whose name I always remember."

As Jemima was about to give herself a metaphorical pat on the back, he added: "I just think to myself, Puddle-Duck."

THE Freecycle website allows people to give their goods away, without charge, to those who want them. We're curious to know if there is a poignant backstory explaining the site's latest offering: Engagement gifts . . . two mugs.

SOME philosophical musings about the fluid nature of identity from reader Andrew Harris, who says: "When you clean out your vacuum cleaner you become a vacuum cleaner."

THE Edinburgh City Police Pipe Band were touring the United States and were about to march on stage with a stirring tune when they heard the MC announce: "Please welcome the Eldinburg Highland Band, from Eldinburg, England."

The band's wounded pride was somewhat soothed by the post-performance hospitality, which arrived in liquid form.

THE news that CalMac's largest and fastest ferry could be out of action for some time has George Dale from Beith wondering if management heads will roll because of the situation.

"Or since it's CalMac," adds George, "perhaps the heads will roll-off then roll-on."

MUSING on all things media related, Stevie Campbell from Hamilton notes that news stories are often based on information gleaned from scientific studies.

"Has any study ever been undertaken to identify the value, or otherwise, of such studies?" asks Stevie.

We're not sure. Though if such a study was devised, wouldn't it then necessitate commissioning a study to ascertain if the study to identify if studies had value was itself worth studying?

Scientific enquiry. It's the slippery slope to insanity.

SLOANS restaurant, working with an organisation called the Scottish Macaroni Appreciation Club (SMAC for short), are selling takeaway dinners called "SMAC in a Box", which is bound to be popular with ravenous Glaswegians.

Though we can't help wondering if some customers might be a tad disappointed upon opening their boxes of SMAC...

WE recall the elderly chap who used to come out with all sorts of muddled malapropisms, and who once said: "I had that appointment at the infirmary yesterday. I was asked to strip off in a cuticle."

TALENTED Diary correspondent Gordon Wright has been a keen musician most of his life, playing guitar and dabbling in percussion. He even bought a set of bongo drums at auction, though later regretted his decision and placed an advert on Gumtree hoping to sell them on.

This resulted in a phone call from a bongo enthusiast. Price was discussed (£20); also condition. The deal was about to be sealed when the buyer enquired about mileage. Gordon

then discovered that Mazda produce a camper van called –
you guessed it – the Bongo.

ANOTHER madcap malapropism. A reader recalls a chap at work saying of someone: "His election address was full of inconstituencies."

A TOILET tale. Fraser Kelly, formerly of the Royal Army Medical Corps, tells us that in the 1980s the parachute regiment dominated Aldershot as their depot was there. For some mysterious reason the other cap badges didn't always see eye-to-eye with the red berets.

Even the upstanding men and women of the Army Medical Services struggled to maintain a civilised relationship with them, which is why, written on the doors of a toilet in the Cambridge military hospital, were the words: "Please flush this toilet hard as it's a long way to the Paras' cookhouse."

WHEN reader Helen Wilson does her weekly shop at the local supermarket she's always quietly amused by the irony of the self-service checkout which invites her to touch the screen to confirm that she wants to pay contactless.

WORKING in Peterhead years ago, George Dale was at a site doing roof repairs. There was a gulls' nest nearby, and the mummy and daddy bird were obviously agitated by our reader's presence, though they never directly approached him. However, George became aware of increasingly frequent, increasingly large, pink deposits of goo landing ever closer to him.

Staring at the strangely coloured blobs, he was overcome by a mixture of curiosity about the birds' diet and concern that the feathered fiends were attempting to use him as an outdoor commode.

His suspicions shifted when he glanced at the guttering below and spotted three fellow workmen. The rascally chaps were entertaining themselves by flicking spoonfuls of strawberry yoghurt in George's direction.

IN the 1980s, reader Athole Fleming worked in advertising sales for a publishing company based in Park Gardens, overlooking Kelvingrove Park. A colleague of Athole's was once gazing out the window and noticed a slender man jogging past. "Look at that," she said with a shudder of distaste. "Ah'v seen mair beef oan a chicken."

ANOTHER cruel description of thin folk. When Tom Stevenson from Stranraer was younger he sometimes heard people of an exceedingly slim stature described as: "A pun o' mince thrown at a skeleton."

A TERRIFYING thought from reader Julie Walton: "If no one can catch the Gingerbread Man, then no one can escape him either . . ."

WE cruelly return to Glasgow epithets inflicted upon skinny chaps. One reader overheard a man being described thus: "He's like a match wi' ra wid scraped aff."

ORCADIAN Willie Towers attended a conference in Mexico where he got into a conversation with a chap from New Zealand, who turned out to be an expat Shetlander.

Willie noticed an American delegate nearby and asked him to join the chat. The American politely declined, explaining: "I'm really sorry, but I don't speak French."

TO get himself in a festive mood during December, Chris Ide from East Renfrewshire bought a Christmas jumper which had a fir tree design with little bulbs. When the battery-powered pack was switched on, the bulbs twinkled merrily. "My son shot a short video clip of this phenomenon," says Chris, "and posted it on our family WhatsApp group." The following day Chris's four-year old grandson proudly announced to his nursery class: "Mummy showed me a video of Grandpa flashing."

ANOTHER memorable phrase used to describe skinny fellows. The mother of Bert Peattie from Kirkcaldy would always say of a slimmer chap: "He's as broad between the shoothers as a kipper between the een."

7

The Bear Necessities

ACCORDING to film website Rotten Tomatoes, *Paddington 2* is one the greatest movies ever made, better even than the classic *Citizen Kane.* Snobbish cinephiles may snarl at this judgement, though the Diary approves. In an era where diversity is demanded of the arts, isn't it high time a flick starring a bear was lauded and applauded?

And aren't our correspondents a little like Paddington, who hails from Peru yet finds himself in a strange, exotic land called the United Kingdom? Our contributors are equally confused and disorientated much of the time. Yet, like Paddington, they courageously do their best and (occasionally) triumph. Some even wear duffel coats and are fond of marmalade sandwiches, though neither are prerequisites of appearing in the Diary.

However, as the following tales make clear, 'bear'-faced cheek is an essential ingredient in most of what we publish . . .

COCKAMAMIE comment time. Reader Arnold Robertson points out: "House flies have existed far longer than houses."

GLOBE-trotting John Dunlop gave a talk about his home nation of Scotland to his grandson's nursery class in New York State. John asked the youngsters if any of their grandparents came from another country. One little hand was thrust eagerly into the air, and a proud voice yelled: "My grandpa's from Minnesota!"

(P.S. And, yes, of course all the children's mums thought our reader was Irish.)

A TORRID tale of a chap shedding his inhibitions. Though in this case the shed-ding is more of a barn-ing. Reader John Mulholland found an old set of quoits in a barn, which he dusted down before challenging his wife to a game in the garden. After he'd won three times in a row, the missus was less than impressed when John turned to her and said, "Post-quoital cigarette, darling?"

THE next season of popular TV show *Line of Duty* will be filmed in Scotland, claims reader Lindsay Young, who adds that we will then discover that the mysterious H, oft mentioned in the show, was in Steps all along.

"I HAVEN'T felt nostalgic in ages," sighs reader Emma Hanley.

CRIME doesn't pay. Unless it's a mega-budget cops-n-robbers TV show. A Hamilton reader has a chum who works at Glasgow Airport. This chap claimed that filming was under-way in the airport shop. Apparently a TV production crew were working on a drama involving cross-border smuggling of wine, spirits and cigarettes.

And the name of the series?

Line of Duty Free.

A PHILOSOPHICAL thought from reader Russell Smith. "The early bird catches the worm," he says. "But isn't it also the early worm that gets caught?"

OUR discussion about the talents of the early bird inspires reader Brian Chrystal to point out: "The early bird may get the worm, but it's the second mouse that gets the cheese."

STUDIES sent to the media invariably highlight very seri-ous subjects. For example, the Diary was contacted about a survey which claimed to have discovered the world's favourite superheroes.

Spider-Man and Batman topped the hero heap, followed by similarly buff boys and girls, all belligerently American.

The Diary demands to know why no Scottish hero made the cut. Where was Likesadramofwhisky-Man?

Or Huddinanumbrellacosit'sfairploochindoonootside-Woman?

Their exclusion should outrage every honourable person who supports truth, justice and the Scottish way.

OFFICIALS at the Tower of London are looking for a name for their new baby corvid, notes a reader. Though they are only allowing people to vote from a selection of boringly predictable names.

"Which is a pity," says our reader. "This would be a great opportunity to remind the world of British eccentricity by calling the bird 'Raven Loony' after the famous political party."

IS the centuries-old hostility between Scotland and England a thing of the past? Have we decided to lay down our claymores and return those clumps of grass, mud and bits of goalpost that we "borrowed" from the Wembley pitch after a 1977 footy victory?

The answer appears to be a resounding . . . mibbe.

For reader John McMenemy has spotted a headline in an English newspaper which triumphantly states: "Sturgeon may find home again in UK after 200-year lull."

Alas, on closer inspection the article turns out to have nothing to do with the mighty Nicola. It's about the slightly less mighty fish that shares her name.

On the plus side, at least we get to keep that forty-year-old Wembley mud.

WE continue devising names for corvids. Reader Alan Thomson, who we assume enjoys the work of gothic horror writer Edgar Allan Poe, says: "Surely an appropriate name for a raven is Quoth?"

THE young son of reader Nicola Gordon complained that he feared sleeping in his attic room as he was afraid of ghosts. Mum responded: "Why would a ghost hang around your attic when there's Netflix and a drinks cabinet in the living room?"

The little chap was satisfied with this answer.

FERRY operator CalMac may have their critics, but when it comes to marketing munchies, they are mighty slick. We hear that they emailed their new lunch menu to interested parties and top of the list was . . . CalMac & Cheese.

TWO refined elderly ladies were overheard gossiping about a mutual friend while on a train from Whitecraigs to Glasgow Central, providing us with the following vignette.

Posh Lady 1: So how much is she drinking?

Posh Lady 2: She's out cold, Doreen. Every single night.

Posh Lady 1: Heavens! So a little bit more than an occasional tippler, would you say?

A READER and his three chums went strolling near Bothwell Castle when they were confronted by a bunch of rowdy local ne'er-do-wells who became very threatening by making an allusion to a famous waterway in Turkey.

"They said that if we didn't vamoose fast, they would boot our Bosphorus," explains our reader.

CURIOUS reader Albert Ross has been thinking about the great innovators of the past. He says: "If the chap who named the walkie-talkie had also named other important inventions, would the kitchen table and chairs now be known as the sittie-eattie?"

THE above tale reminds us that the French refuse to refer to the contraption in question as a walkie-talkie.

Instead, they call it 'un talkie-walkie'.

(Clearly the French Revolution didn't sate our Gallic neighbour's hunger for rebellious behaviour.)

SPORTS fan Oliver Hall persuaded his theatre-loving girlfriend to watch a game of footy on the telly.

"Never again," shudders Oliver, who adds: "When a player came off the bench she said: 'Is that the understudy?'"

WITH age comes wisdom. But what else does it bring? A reader says: "When I was young, I was poor. But after years of hard, honest, painstaking work . . . I am no longer young."

GLASGOW rock musician Bobby Gillespie surprisingly revealed he wants the Italian actress Monica Bellucci to play him if a biographical film is made of his life.

Reader Scott Sharp says: "If that sort of flexibility is allowed in the casting process, I'm now eagerly anticipating Meryl Streep as the lead in *The Alex Salmond Story*."

A HELPFUL comment from reader Neil Murray: "Never trust an electrician with frizzy hair."

WE wonder who should play Alex Salmond in a movie of his life. "Obviously Shrek," chuckles reader Margaret Thomson. We assume because the animated ogre, like Mr Salmond, has a Scottish accent and an all-consuming fondness for his native land. Nothing to do with his appearance, of course.

IT appears that the citizens of Muirend have decided to dilly-dally inside the mind of Salvador Dalí. Local chap Bill Harvey witnessed the surreal sight of a group of elderly residents whose wobbly bits were sloshing about in Lycra as they gasped and groaned their way through an exercise class in a gym car park.

"If the keep-fit crew are impinging on the territory of cars,"

says Bill, "shouldn't the cars be allowed into the human fief-
dom of the gym? I'm sure the BMWs and Minis would love
a shot on the running machines."

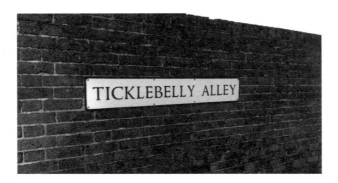

THE Diary isn't merely a source of delight and entertainment. We also help our readers navigate the choppy waters
of existence. We are a lighthouse of wisdom; a beacon shining brightly to aid weary travellers in need of safe harbour
from the vagaries and tragedies of life.

In our ever-present manner of helpfulness, a reader
observes: "Never trust a plumber wearing wellies and overalls
sponsored by Vileda."

LATEST government health advice reminds a Lanarkshire
reader of a static caravan holiday he endured in a sabbath-
observant island. No newspapers, poor TV reception, wind
and rain aplenty. Though he did unearth a book which, to
his delight and anticipation, was named *How to Hug*.

He was crestfallen to discover it was an overdue library
book that was one volume of an encyclopaedia.

NOSTALGIC reader Martina Long says: "You know you're old when you dust to the music you once danced to."

YEARS ago reader Martin Garfield worked at a gym famous for training Scottish boxers. He recalls two lumpy lads getting in the ring to have a practice punch-up.

One lumpy lad walloped the other square in the face, causing the victim's nose to gush with blood.

"Yuv broken ma nostril," howled this poor chap.

To which the other combatant responded incredulously: "Ye cannae break a nostril, ya numpty. It's a hole. Like the stuff in the middle of a donut."

"With chat like that," says Martin, "I fully understood why they preferred to knock lumps out of each other."

CONFUSED reader Brian Hall was browsing in a supermarket when he noticed a new variety of those popular crisps in a tube, which was labelled "Pulled Pork Burger".

"Since when did 'pulling' become a flavour?" enquires Brian, who adds: "When I played tug-of-war as a kid, I don't remember the pastime having a distinctive taste."

SCOTTISH education remains unrivalled, argues reader Mary Fraser, who informed her teenage niece that she was seeing a chiropractor.

"Isn't that some kind of dinosaur?" enquired the niece.

8

Punk, Penicillin & Potato Scones

THE Diary has many fond memories of Una Stubbs, who sadly died in Edinburgh last August. The actress proved herself to be a miracle worker early in her career by being just about the only person to ever make Cliff Richard look cool, when she starred alongside him in the movie *Summer Holiday*.

Cliff was too stiff a quiff to compete with Elvis, but by hanging out with Una on the big screen he showed us all that he had something going for him.

Stubbs was also memorable in the sitcom *Till Death Us Do Part* and became known to a whole new generation for her quirky and lovable turn as Mrs Hudson in *Sherlock*.

The Diary most fondly recalls her performance in *Worzel Gummidge*. This was wooden acting of the highest calibre. (She played Aunt Sally, a wooden fairground doll come to life.) Few public figures were so versatile. Few will be so sadly missed.

Though there are some performers and sportsmen who were in her league, who we also lost during the last twelve months.

Each of these stars was truly unique. Or should that be Una-ique?

Here's our recollections of a few of them . . .

A CURIOUS sighting in Edinburgh, where the bat-signal is spotted glowing on the side of the King's Theatre. Is Batman in town, ignoring social-distancing rules in order to punch miscreants squarely on the jaw? Not quite.

The projection is in memory of Andy Gray, who has sadly died. The comic actor, who regularly played the King's, was a huge fan of the Caped Crusader.

Andy was also known to be a bit of a superhero himself. His special power was the ability to make audiences roar with laughter.

Which beats X-Ray vision and bullet-proof skin any day of the week.

ANDY Gray could always grab a giggle from an audience and those he worked with. Fellow performer Iain Johnstone starred alongside Andy in what he describes as: "One of the worst shows ever to have disgraced the Scottish stage."

He realised he had a chum in the cast during the first day's read-through when he became aware of Andy's pen repeatedly tapping the table in the following pattern: Dot, dot, dot. Dash, dash, dash. Dot, dot, dot.

It was spelling SOS in morse code.

Looking Andy square in the eye, Iain lifted his own pen . . . and started tapping.

ANOTHER Andy Gray yarn. Reader Tim Huntingford spent an evening in a Perth watering hole with the comedy great, who was appearing in a local theatre. The pub was full of Welsh rugby fans, up for a game at Murrayfield. Andy and Tim got chatting to two Welsh women.

On being introduced to Andy, the ladies somehow managed to confuse him with that other legendary Andy Gray.

The one who played footy for Scotland.

Andy decided not to disabuse them of this notion.

For the rest of the evening he gave a virtuoso performance as a quality kickabout king.

FELLOW actor Jonathan Watson stood next to Andy Gray in a long queue that at first glance looked like an identity parade at the local cop shop.

On further examination it turned out to be a line of celebrities waiting to bow and curtsey to a royal dignitary after a theatrical performance.

Unfortunately, Andy and Jonathan happened to be a tad squiffy, which might not have gone down well with the blue blood in attendance.

Luckily it happened to be Princess Margaret, who was never a stickler for royal protocol.

Luckier still, she gave the impression that she was even more bladdered than the lads.

GERRY Marsden was one of the most likable rockers of the swinging sixties, and the populariser of that classic song 'You'll Never Walk Alone' which Celtic fans love to warble.

Gerry and his band the Pacemakers were chums of The Beatles, and the Diary recalls the occasion when both groups, still to find fame, played Hamburg.

Gerry and John Lennon, out strolling one day, came across a house of ill repute which took their fancy. They scraped together enough money to enjoy the services provided and entered the place, where they were confronted by a lady of the night who bore a startling resemblance to an outhouse of the sturdy brick variety.

Terrified, the rockers fled.

Gerry later complained to John that it had been a waste of money, adding: "We got nothing."

John replied: "I did. I got the fright of me bloody life."

THE Diary was sad to hear of the death of country crooner Sydney Devine, a performer with a huge fan base who never took himself too seriously.

It was a longstanding Scottish tradition to poke fun at his musical abilities, though he was revered in certain quarters.

There can't be many popular entertainers who have poems named after them, but Sydney did.

Dumbarton FC's poet-in-residence, Stephen Watt, once wrote a verse celebrating Alba's musical heritage. The stirring ode was grandly titled: 'Scottish Elements Are Conceived from the Glitter of Sydney Devine's Tour Jacket'.

WE continue remembering the late singer Sydney Devine. Broadcaster Tony Currie used to work with the country crooner when they both presented shows at Radio Clyde. One day Sydney came into the studio in a state of some excitement, carrying a reel of tape containing the backing tracks for an album he was making called *Doubly Devine*.

"You've got to hear these, Tony, they're brilliant," enthused Sydney, adding: "I want you to hear them before I spoil them by singing over the tracks."

ANOTHER Sydney Devine memory. Reader Stanley Milton says: "I remember it being said of Sydney that he didn't release records, they escaped."

SYDNEY was once approached by a worthy at his local golf club, who asked if the country crooner was aware of the monthly social evenings.

Sydney admitted that he was.

"And you know we're always looking for talented entertainers?" said the worthy.

"Yes," nodded Sydney, in a 'Go on, ask if you must' sort of tone.

"Well," said the worthy, "do you know any?"

ON the popular STV music show *Thingummyjig* presenter Jack McLaughlin would always introduce Sydney as: "The Cleland Cowboy who has been thrown off more stages than John Wayne."

A FORMER Edinburgh GP recalls that when the first drugs for HIV and AIDS were prescribed in the 1980s some patients struggled with the pharmacological names Zidovudine and Lamivudine.

So they became known as "Sydney Devine" and "Lami Devine".

COMEDY writer Ian Pattison recalls one of his personal heroes, Liverpool footballer Ian St John. "As a kid I sent my autograph book to him at Liverpool, hoping for his signature," says Ian. "About a week later the book arrived back in an envelope reeking of wintergreen. He'd passed the book round the entire dressing room and had them all sign. Roger Hunt, Ian Callaghan, Ron Yeats, Chris Lawler, the lot."

Yeats and Saint had even flicked through the book and signed the Dundee United and Motherwell pages too, being former players.

"Best of it is," chuckles Ian, "I was a cheap little b*****d and hadn't even put a stamp on the envelope."

MORE fond memories of Ian St John. Reader Larry Hutchison says the Liverpool striker's legendary status with club supporters was neatly encapsulated when the poster for a local evangelical revivalist campaign was displayed with the challenging headline: "What Will You Do When the Lord Returns to Earth?"

This resulted in the graffiti response: "Move St John to Inside-Forward."

AS we mentioned previously, the Duke of Edinburgh also sadly died this year. He was an often irascible, yet eminently relatable chap. Reader Stuart Swanston recalls that when Prince Philip was Chancellor of the University of Edinburgh in the 1970s he opened a new building in the Zoology department.

After unveiling a plaque, he was shown round the labs where he noticed a molecular biologist who, being an ardent republican, had boycotted the opening ceremony. This fellow was bent over a microscope, tweezers in hand.

Prince Philip strode over and enquired what he was doing.

"I was counting the bristles on the legs of drosophila – that's fruit flies to you – and you've just made me lose count," snapped the scientist.

Prince Philip retorted: "And I'm just doing my bloody job, too."

THE Duke of Edinburgh's death reminds a retired Glasgow teacher of the unique outdoor initiative he instigated, which often became a handy excuse used by pupils who failed to produce homework.

"Aw miss, ah wis away daein' ma chookie embra," they would say.

"Even the staff who led such excursions would refer to a 'chookie weekend'," recalls our correspondent.

WE'VE pointed out that Prince Philip inspired teens with his Duke of Edinburgh's Award initiative. Though it wasn't only youngsters he helped.

Retired politician Dennis Canavan recalls that the February 1974 General Election produced a hung parliament. William Baxter MP opined that the country should be ruled by a council of state consisting of representatives from every major party. When asked by an interviewer who should preside over this council, Baxter replied: "Somebody neutral, like Prince Philip."

This triggered demands for Baxter's resignation. He eventually acquiesced and Dennis was selected to succeed him at the following General Election.

"So Prince Philip inadvertently kick-started my political career!" chuckles Dennis.

BAY City Rollers fan Jenny Murphy mourns the death of the band's frontman Les McKeown. Our reader points out that although the Edinburgh outfit played bubblegum pop, they also provided the inspiration for grittier grooves, with original New York punk rockers, the Ramones, admitting they found inspiration from a Rollers song.

"So Scotland invented punk, penicillin and potato scones," says Jenny. "The world owes us so much."

TOMMY Docherty wasn't just a football manager. He also moonlighted as a wit, a wag and a warper of words. When Tommy was in charge of Preston North End a journalist asked him to describe the team's position as they struggled to escape relegation.

"We're on the crest of a slump," admitted Tommy.

DOCHERTY once found himself managing Scotland's national team, who were to play Sweden. Having assiduously done his homework, he delivered a team talk to his defenders. Which is when he offered them the excellent advice to: "Jist watch the big blond fella."

IN the 1960s football transfer fees were rocketing and had reached the precipitous peak of £100,000. (Roughly the amount modern players shell out on laces for their new trainers.)

A popular English striker named Tony Hateley (father of Mark) was making headlines at the time and Tommy Docherty was asked how much he thought he was worth.

"A hundred thousand wouldn't buy him," said Tommy, who then added: "And I'm one of them."

TOMMY was interviewed on TV in the 1970s at a football ground where the crowd had rioted. "What should be done to stop this?" asked the interviewer.

"Bring back capital punishment," was Tommy's response.

"Don't you mean corporal punishment?" the flummoxed reporter stuttered.

"Call it what you want," said Tommy. "They've got to bring it back."

DURING another TV interview about violence on the football terraces, Tommy announced in magisterial tones: "See this hooliganism? I could half the problem by seventy-five per cent."

TOMMY was a manager whose quips often had more quality than the players he fielded. Recalling his time in charge of Rotherham United, he said: "I promised I would take Rotherham out of the Second Division, and I took them into the Third. The old chairman said: 'Doc, you're a man of your word.'"

A TALE of unfettered nudity. David Miller from Milngavie recalls the chap who pranced across a fairway, sans clothing, during a golf tournament.

The late sports commentator Peter Alliss, famed as a witty wag, said of the wicked wagger: "What a lot of fuss about a little thing like that."

9

Are You Being Served?

DIARY contributors are often confronted by waiting staff whose finesse does not impress. Our readers always have the option to complain about poor service before they settle the bill, though many prefer to be discreet and bite their tongue. (Sometimes that's the tastiest food available.)

Only later do they report their dire dining experiences by getting in touch with the Diary.

The following chapter includes the choicest morsels from the banquet of despair that our readers have provided us with as they dish the dirt on dodgy dishes.

So brace yourself, because these foody tales are hard to swallow. Quite frankly, that's just the way we like 'em . . .

A POSH banquet was taking place in Glasgow when one of the guests requested a portion of spinach with his main course.

"Certainly sir," replied the waiter.

Unfortunately, the main course arrived minus the spinach. Though shortly afterwards, a less than obsequious waitress appeared with a bowl of the green stuff.

Not sure who had ordered it, she growled: "Which wan o' youse is Popeye?"

FEELING rather parched, reader Gordon Casely and his wife stopped for a coffee in the heart of Aberdeenshire and ordered: "Twa coffees an twa butteries." (Explanation for the uninitiated: A buttery is fit they cry a savoury bread roll in Aiberdeen.)

The waitress returned with the coffee and butteries. She then groped around in her armpit before producing two packets of butter, very recently deep-frozen, but now thawing out nicely.

BACK in the late 1970s reader Jack Davidson was dining in a fairly smart Dumfries restaurant. One of the company, having never heard of a certain item on the menu, asked the waiter what *calzone* was. This prompted the response: "Eh . . . it's kinda like . . . uh . . . an Italian Forfar bridie."

VISITING a theatre bar, reader Bob Byiers requested two glasses of red wine, then asked if there was a choice. The barman proudly replied: "Yes. Large or small."

PETER Mackay from Kincraig admired the skills of a serving wench who was handing out soup at a swanky event. The choice was Scotch broth or consommé, so the lady toddled round the tables asking diners if they would have: "Thick or thin?"

THE vegetarian diet does not appeal to everyone. A reader recalls a useful tip he received for cooking kale: "Always add a large dash of olive oil to your kale. It makes it so much easier to scrape off the plate."

A LADY was with some colleagues at a restaurant table when the waitress, clearing up, asked her to pass "that bowl, please".

The lady tried to help, though with her hand hovering over the table, was forced to say: "Er, there isn't a bowl on the table."

Patiently the waitress explained: "The sauce boa'll, the sauce boa'll."

THE Diary's culinary correspondent David Donaldson notes that insect-derived protein has been given the go-ahead for human consumption. "How long will it be before we start seeing packets of Mincey Wincy on our supermarket shelves?" he wonders.

SOME chaps were enjoying a meal in a Campbeltown Indian restaurant where the waitress's whiplash tongue was notorious. Perusing the menu, one of the chaps asked this lady: "What's naan bread?"

Rolling her eyes, she replied: "Indian loaf, bawheid."

ATTEMPTING to enjoy dinner in a Stewarton hotel, a chap asked the waitress for his steak to be cooked very rare.

Scrunching up her face, she replied: "Oooh. All that blood. Disgusting!"

ALTHOUGH we're enjoying a sly chuckle at the expense of waiting staff, reader John Hart reminds us that customers also have their calamitous moments.

One of John's friends went on a first date as a teenager and splashed out on a posh restaurant. After this naive young fellow had ordered steak, the waiter enquired how he'd like it done.

"Grilled?" came the hopeful reply.

ANOTHER tale involving waiting staff whose lack of sophistication led to customer protestation. John Haddow from Dunblane was once in an Alloa café. A woman at the next table called the young waitress over to point out that the cup of coffee she had just served had lipstick on the rim.

The waitress picked up the cup, examined it, then said with a cheerful laugh: "That's no' lipstick. I cut my finger."

VISITING a restaurant many years ago, reader Tony Grant overheard a customer at a nearby table being asked how he would like his steak.

"Just like winning an argument with my wife," replied the chap.

The waiter nodded knowingly, then said: "Rare it is, sir."

ENJOYING a meal in a swanky Glasgow restaurant, Gordon Fisher from Stewarton was rather startled when a large and rough-looking chap emitted an indecorous noise from his nether regions.

A woman at an adjacent table glowered at her husband and cocked her head in the direction of the culprit. The timid-looking husband cleared his throat and said in the firmest voice he could muster: "Excuse me, you broke wind in front of my wife."

To which the offender gallantly replied: "Am sorry, pal. Ah didnae know she wanted tae go first."

FOOD is much more sophisticated abroad. George MacDougall from Edinburgh recalls his first trip to Paris in 1950. Happy to leave ration-book Britannia far behind, he and a chum visited a plush eatery in swanky Montmartre.

George was delighted to spot steak on the menu, and indulged himself in the meaty treat.

"That's the best bit of beef I've ever eaten," he told his pal, who raised a quizzical eyebrow.

"That wasn't beef," explained the pal. "It was horse."

READER Robert Gardner once attended the funeral of a chap he had known. Many of the mourners had journeyed great distances to pay their respects, and a meal at a local hotel was provided. While everyone was enjoying some friendly banter a waitress asked the diners if they wanted chicken, steak or the vegan option. The gentleman next to Robert requested steak. Asked how he would like it, he said: "Just wipe its a**e and put it on the plate."

After a dignified silence, the waitress replied: "That will be rare, then."

WE hear that the Thornwood Bar in Dumbarton Road has outraged sensitive members of its gourmet-gobbling clientele by serving chips in a mug.

Though some customers are positively enthusiastic, with one impressed diner stating that he now eagerly anticipates hot dogs served in slippers.

A SCOTTISH chap was once presented with two large, meaty delicacies in a Spanish restaurant. The waiter sated the diner's curiosity by informing him that they were a bull's bobbly bits.

Some days later the chap was presented with two much smaller hunks of meat in the same restaurant.

With a resigned shrug, the waiter said: "Sometimes, the bull, he win."

10
A Spooky Interlude

With a Shivery Short Story We Call . . .
The Provan Hall Mystery
(Starring the Herald Diary's Brave Editor
plus a host of other kooks and spooks)

Chapter the First
In Which Our Hero Makes a Gruesome Discovery

TO quote that great scholar of the paranormal, Scooby Doo: "Yoikes!"

Like Mr Doo throughout most of his illustrious ghost-hunting career, I find myself in a spot of bother at present.

The night is dark and dismal. I'm standing on the outskirts of nowhere. On my own.

No, not quite alone.

I have the howling wind and crooked trees for company.

And the wind gossips its terrible secrets to those trees, and the trees reply by shaking their palsied, arthritic branches in merriment.

In front of me looms Provan Hall. The fifteenth-century building in Easterhouse's Auchinlea Park has a reputation for being one of the most haunted houses in Scotland.

I've arranged to meet a gang of ghost hunters here, though not a ghost hunter do I see.

Rattling the tall gates that block my entrance to the driveway, I shout in a voice I wish sounded bolder: "Hello? Anybody there?"

The wind answers with an exalted whoop. Nobody else does. With quivering fingers I tap out a message on my mobile phone to Julia Girdwood, my principal contact in the ghost-hunter community.

"Hi, Julia. I'm at Provan Hall. There doesn't seem to be anyone around . . ."

A few moments later I receive a text back. "Lorne. The event's tomorrow night."

Oops.

Chapter the Second
In Which More Discoveries Are Made,
Hideous and Otherwise

YOIKES!

It's a few minutes to midnight, the following evening. I'm

crouching in the dark on the top floor of Provan Hall, when David, the professional medium standing next to me, says in a matter-of-fact voice: "There's a crawler coming up the stairs."

A w-w-what?!

I glance over at the stairs. With only the dim glow from David's torch, I make out shadows and nothing more. But David, being a medium, claims to be in possession of special powers. Ghosts are visible to him, he says, and they often tell him their tragic stories. He sometimes glimpses demons, too. They're less sympathetic entities, as you'd imagine. The thing climbing the stairs towards us would appear to be of their ilk.

Since I can't see it, I'm understandably curious to know what this crawler looks like. Does it slither on flailing tentacles, or scuttle on a multitude of twitching legs?

"It looks sort of like Gollum," clarifies David, referring to the malicious creature from *Lord of the Rings*.

David works with a group called Scottish Ghost Nights, which organises a variety of spooky events throughout the country. They hold seances and late-night vigils in castles, derelict jails and stately homes.

For tonight's proceedings the creepy quotient should be high, for it's only a few days before Halloween and Provan Hall has a distinctive ambience. Imagine you're Hansel or Gretel, trudging through the tangled forest of your worst nightmares, when you stumble upon a sturdy, ancient house where a sweet old pensioner lives. And – oh joy! – her cooking pot's on the boil. Must be something yummy for dinner . . .

Provan Hall has a similar occult energy to that old pensioner's gaff, though it's built of sullen stone, not candy.

It's a squatting toad of a house. Bathed in the clear autumn moonlight, its walls are bone-bland, pockmarked and bled of lustre, like the powdered face of a diseased French aristocrat awaiting Madame Guillotine.

And I'm hunkered down inside that house, along with my new chum, David, another medium called Natasha, plus an assortment of ghost hunters and ghoul groupies, who paid to be here tonight, desperate to be scared witless.

There's twenty of us in total. Mostly women, with the occasional fear-loving fellow thrown into the mix.

As the night progresses, Natasha also glimpses a demon, which she describes as looking like a "barbecued monkey with not very nice eyes".

David chimes in, too. "It's a shape-shifter," he says. "And it can climb the walls."

Regrettably, once again I fail to glimpse this demon. Though being partial to anything barbecued, I do start to feel rather peckish.

Luckily, the ghost hunters have brought along scrummy cakes in Tupperware boxes, and we all have a hearty munch during a well-earned break.

To be honest, I'm not really feeling the creeping sense of

unease I experienced the night before, when I arrived early and alone.

It's hard to get a satisfying shiver snaking down your spine when you're in the company of a bunch of good-natured, cheerful ghost hunters. We're all having a grand old time of it, you see, and that's a bit of a problem. A gaggle of giggling girls are on one side of me. Hen-night happy, hen-night hysterical.

Also, many paying guests are wearing woolly hats topped with pom-poms. I mean, come on, guys! Would Jack Nicholson have been half as terrifying in *The Shining* if he'd swapped his axe and manic grin for a pom-pom hat?

Yvonne, one of the ghost hunters, explains that there's nothing wrong with boisterous energy when searching for otherworldly entities. High spirits can persuade other types of spirits to make contact.

Like most of the professionals here tonight, Yvonne declines to allow me to use her surname in print. She doesn't want daylight acquaintances knowing her night-time occupation. For all that, she's an earthy sort, with nothing remotely mysterious or ethereal about her personality.

"Shout out to the spirits if you want," she tells me. "Don't worry about sounding like a bit of a tool."

Another ghost hunter, Eva, agrees. "Think of tonight like a party," she says. "You've got to be single and ready to mingle. If you just stand in a corner, quiet and shy, the spirits won't be energised enough to make contact."

Chapter the Third
Of Witches, Maidens and Dastardly Monks

SO our group does its best to encourage ghosts, ghoulies and other ghastlies to get in touch. We're asked to briskly rub our hands together, to build up energy in the room. We also shout out questions to the invisible spirits surrounding us.

"We are your friends," says David. "We have as much to learn from you, as you do from us."

Little rubber balls are placed on the floor. They're called kitten balls, rather incongruously, and when they are moved, they strobe flashing lights, like 1970s disco balls. Shouting out questions, we encourage the spirits to answer us by shifting these little balls.

Occasionally a flash of light does spark through the darkness, indicating the balls are on the go. Conclusive evidence ghosts exist? I'm not convinced. Most likely it's evidence we're standing in a draughty old house with rickety floorboards, where rubber balls are apt to wobble.

We try a variety of other gizmos and gadgets to get in touch with the other side.

A Ouija board. No luck.

Then a contraption that emits strange screeches and crackles. Voices from the other side or radio interference?

Once again, I'm not persuaded.

A red light is used to illuminate the faces of various

members of our group. If those faces morph into something different, it means a spirit is standing in front of that person. And, yes, faces do change. Sort of. Though only because the light teases shadows from the contours of noses, foreheads and mouths.

The two spiritualists in our group spot more uncanny happenings. Ghosts of small children brush past, telling tales of a drowning in a pond. A hanged man swings from a banister. A pentagram on the kitchen flagstones marks the spot where a witch once worshipped. Nearby a wretched maiden was groped by a gang of dastardly monks.

I glimpse none of this, however. Only the mediums see all.

Julia Girdwood, who's in charge of the evening, tells me events aren't always dramatic, scary or opinion-shifting when it comes to believing (or not) in ghosts.

"We don't fake anything," she says. "Which means the nights vary. People sometimes come away a bit disappointed when things are quiet. Or they have a genuine uncanny experience."

Speaking of which, did I come to believe, at night's end, that Provan Hall is haunted? I'm afraid that, although I enjoyed the evening (and cake), I left forming a conclusion familiar to many a courthouse jury.

Spooks in the house? Verdict: Not Provan.

11
The Job Lot

THE passing fads of pop culture leave the Diary cold. Our preference is to don a smoking jacket, wind up the gramophone, then relax in a well-stuffed easy chair next to a roaring log fire while the timeless tunes of Beethoven and Brahms dissolve us into a state of reverie.

Which is why we were surprised back in February to find ourselves extoling the virtues of Posh Spice, when she was auctioned for £262,000. A hefty sum, though apparently her value was thanks to reduced-fat cover and meat tenderness.

On further investigation it transpired that Posh Spice was actually "Poshspice", a Shropshire cow sold at market.

Nevertheless, there's surely a moral to this story. Every single one of us has value, even if that value can only be measured in steaks and chops.

Many people find their greatest sense of worth in the career they choose.

The following tales focus on people attempting to do their jobs, though we must warn you that sometimes a career can easily career out of control . . .

WE are told of a chap who taught in a large secondary school in Glasgow's Southside many years ago.

For a treat this fellow took the top pupils in his class to Blair Drummond Safari Park. As fourteen of the Sooside's brightest scholars relaxed on the grass, contemplating life and puffing fags, the tranquillity was disturbed by an irate park ranger. With gun fully cocked, he screamed: "Get back on your bus NOW. There's lions everywhere! Get back on your bus NOW."

Whereupon one of the pupils, who just might have been a prefect, shouted at the ranger: "Calm doon, ya rocket. Nae-body's touchin' yer f***in' lions."

[116]

READERS will be aware that Higher English pupils must provide a folio of their own original writing. We recall one young English scholar in a school in Glasgow's East End who showed scant interest in the course. He also had no talent for creative writing, yet somehow managed to submit an outstanding extract from a short story he claimed was his own.

Teacher, smelling a rat, took a segment from the story and ran it through Google Advanced search. Within seconds Google concluded that the tale was the work of a certain Stephen King, bestselling author.

Our teacher challenged the young scholar, and asked if he had anything to say for himself.

Quick as a flash, he replied: "Aye. I cannae believe that b*****d stole ma story."

MORE classroom plagiarism. Retired teacher Tony Skarratt recalls a mischievous young student who handed in a short story that was suspiciously similar to the movie *Planet of the Apes*. Our reader pointed this out to the pupil, who was understandably outraged that his artistic integrity had been questioned.

"It's no' the same ata'," grumbled the aggrieved author. "Ma story's called *Planet o' the Monkeys*. An' monkeys urnie apes."

ONE of our readers taught in Easterhouse before retirement. He recalls a young scholar proudly revealing that he had been reading *Oliver Twist* in his spare time, and particularly liked the "Arthur" Dodger character.

When teacher explained that it was the Artful Dodger, the scholar looked baffled.

"You sure that isnae a printin' mistake?" he countered. "A dinnae hink Artful's a boy's name."

MORE twist-ed tales from *Oliver*. Retired high school teacher Gordon Fisher from Stewarton explains that as part of their English studies, his S1s were encouraged (i.e. telt) to choose a book from the school library and write a review about it.

One ambitious fellow chose *Oliver Twist*. The concerned teacher explained to his pupil that this was a rather weighty tome, so perhaps he should choose something on the lighter side, as only one week was allocated to the task.

The scholar was undaunted and assured his teacher that all would be fine.

The essay was duly submitted, containing the highly insightful introductory sentence: *"Oliver Twist* by Charles Dickens was really good and how he managed to put all those great songs in it was amazing!"

THINKING about the arcane mysteries of the binary system reminds Grant MacKenzie from Bearsden of an ex-maths teacher colleague who tested his pupils' knowledge by writing the following statement on the blackboard: "There are only ten kinds of people in the world – those who under-stand binary, and those who don't."

THE advent of Standard Grade meant pupils were allowed to use dictionaries in exams. After sitting his prelim for German, one young scholar bitterly complained to teacher Barrie Crawford that he couldn't find any of the words he was looking for in his dictionary. On investigation, Barrie discovered that the lad was using a French dictionary.

Sacré bleu! (Or do we mean *Scheisse?*)

A LANGUAGE teacher recalls a young scholar in his charge who produced the following sentence in his German home-work: "*In der Schule studiere ich Englisch, Mathe und Friedhof.*"

Teutonic linguists among our readers will have translated this as: "At school I study English, maths and graveyard."

The language teacher puzzled over this mysterious sen-tence for a while, then realised his pupil had wanted to write "chemistry".

Unable to spell the word in English, he had instead stum-bled upon "cemetery" in his English/German dictionary.

A RETIRING teacher informed his class that, having completed over twenty-five years in education, he would be quitting in a few months.

One of his pupils raised a hand in response to this momen-tous news.

"Yes, Hector?" said the teacher, who believed that an appreciative send-off was about to take place.

"Does that mean we're going to get a proper teacher, then?" asked the pupil.

Bless them, sighed the teacher. Such inquiring little minds.

A GLASGOW high school teacher was delivering a Zoom tutorial to her pupils, who were all learning from home.

At a crucial point in the lesson one of the boys in the class revealed that he needed to visit the toilet. Intent on not missing any part of his education, he added: "Don't worry. I'll take you along with me."

He then picked up his laptop and strolled towards the toilet while his horrified teacher and the other students screamed: "No! Switch off! Switch off!"

A HIGH school instructor from Edinburgh gets in touch to relate a similarly painful tale to the one above.

This fine educator was also teaching a class using Zoom technology, and she found herself berating her students.

"Look at you all," she snarled. "When I'm talking I don't see anyone taking notes. And not one of you has put up a hand to ask a question. Honestly, there's just no engagement at all . . ."

As the teacher continued to scold her pupils, one of them managed to say: "Um, miss. You do know you're on mute?"

ANOTHER of our fine but frazzled educators managed to escape the torments and terrors of the teaching profession by making the decision to retire. It was a month before she revealed the news to the little scamps – sorry, splendid prodigies – in her charge.

One girl responded by saying she already realised big changes were afoot, explaining: "You smiled wan day."

AFTER a long teaching career, Al Reid concluded that he had performed the same song and dance routine in front of thousands of pupils, so decided to retire. Word quickly got round and a senior pupil interrupted one of his final lessons by politely enquiring what his future plans were. Al jokingly replied that he was thinking of going on the stand-up circuit.

"Well," the pupil said thoughtfully. "You'll need some new material, then."

THE longest running war in human history is between teachers and parents. Reader Margaret Thomson recalls a new family moving into her area, followed by the mother bringing the daughter to enrol at the primary school.

After the head teacher had shown Mum round, the head said: "Don't worry. Your daughter will soon settle in and enjoy being here."

Mum was outraged by such a wicked suggestion.

"She's no here tae enjoy hersel'," she scolded the foolish head teacher. "She's here tae get learnt."

SOLICITOR Matthew Berlow, who tinkles the ivories in his spare time, believes he may be the only lawyer to have played piano in a legal setting.

"Helensburgh Justice of the Peace Court used to be held in an old church hall," he explains. "And the piano was still there. So I started to play and was concentrating so hard I didn't realise court had started."

Matthew was representing Faslane protestors at the time, who threatened to bring their guitars to any further court appearance for a stirring collaboration with their lawyer of 'Give Peace a Chance'.

AN English teacher based in Glasgow's West End was explaining to her class that there used to be grammar exams.

One proud pupil piped up: "Oh, I know grammar! I had a teacher who used to talk it all the time."

LANGUAGES teacher Moira Campbell was once doing a vocab test and asked her class to write down the French word for tap.

One little fellow thrust his hand in the air and enquired: "The wan the watter comes out of, or the tap o' yer heid?"

A TEACHER recalls a student's wonky translation from German into English, where the original German sentence had the meaning of: "Father went quickly into the bathroom and turned on the light."

This was rather freely adapted into: "Father ran into the bathroom at the speed of light."

JUST in case you think we should pity pupils instead of pillorying them, here's a tale of how dastardly young scholars can be.

A friend of reader Brendan Keenan is a retired head teacher. He tells the story of a former pupil, turned bald and bearded, who was invited to speak at his alma mater.

Ignoring teacherly advice, he asked the pupils if they had any questions, which led to the immediate response: "Mister, is yer heid oan upside down?"

WE recall the high school scholar who was working on an essay in German about her home life. She mentioned having a cat, then revealed that she regularly fed it.

Unfortunately, she chose the wrong German verb, which resulted in her admitting that she had been breastfeeding the poor moggie.

RETIRED high school teacher Marvin Hollis always enjoyed visiting his local theatre in the past, especially when he used to bring along his classes from Glasgow's East End.

He recalls watching the balcony scene from *Romeo and Juliet* with his pupils. The drama on stage was reaching its crescendo when one young lad cried out: "Gon yersel, Romeo. Dinnae be faffin', noo!"

PILOT Doug Maughan once arrived at Heathrow Airport. Resplendent in his BA captain's uniform, he strode past a crowd of passengers, just off a flight from Glasgow.

One young lad shouted excitedly: "Dad, look, it's a pirate!"

"Ah, if only," sighed Doug. "They have better hats."

A FLIGHT of fancy is provided by one of our readers, a former pilot. "How do you know someone's a pilot?" he asks. "Because it's the first thing he says to you."

MORE about those magnificent men in their flying machines. "Some people say pilots are incapable of feelings of empathy, intimacy and affection," says a reader who used to be one. "But that's not true. It's just that those feelings don't involve anyone else."

A GLASGOW bloke discovered he had been picked for jury duty. The fellow explained to the legal authorities that he couldn't possibly accept this important public responsibility as he had already sat on a jury sometime before.

Later he was thinking about his time in court and realised how strange it had been, with famous faces galore and TV cameras pointing in every direction. Eventually the penny dropped and he realised his memory was utterly muddled.

The jury he had sat on was when he played an extra in a court scene of the soap opera *River City*.

PLANES used to make brief refuelling stops on long journeys, a former pilot tells us. On one occasion a blind man and his dog were in the cabin.

The captain decided to take the dog for a short walk while the aircraft was being refuelled. Which was kind of him. Though you can imagine the consternation among passengers with a window seat, who happened to spy their pilot wearing dark glasses while walking round the aircraft clutching the harness of a guide dog.

A FORMER pilot recalls one captain's party piece. While his plane was airborne, this chap would emerge from the flight deck unrolling two long pieces of string. He'd then go up to an unsuspecting passenger seated in the front row of the cabin, offer them the two ends of string, then request that they work the controls while he popped to the loo.

IN the era before computers and email, unlucky teachers would sometimes discover a slip of paper in their staffroom dookit. This form was known as a YUFTI, which translated as "yufti" take another class. The necessary details began with the expression "please take".

A teacher from Stewarton recalls a Monday morning when there had been a terrible outbreak of hangovers (sorry, serious illness) in his school. A frazzled depute was frantically trying to cover the necessary classes.

Our teacher didn't ease the depute's stress when he handed back his "please take" emblazoned with the words: "No thanks."

The depute shot our teacher an angry glare, who responded by using an expression he had learned from an S3 girl.

"Sakes man," said he. "Can you no' take a joke?"

Apparently he couldn't.

HIJINKS on the high seas. When Dave Poole from Appin in Argyll was in the merchant navy he sailed with a Danish engineer named Hans Neesan, who could never understand why the British officers chose to call him 'Boomps-a-daisy'.

THINKING about the ferocity of some ferry jaunts, Robin Johnston from Newton Mearns recalls Captain "Squeaky" Smith, a well-known CalMac skipper of yesteryear, who was once buffeted by a storm of such severity that a passenger implored the Lord to send his son to save everyone on the boat.

Squeaky Smith decided to interject. "Dear Lord," he said. "Dinna send your son. Come yourself. It's no work for a boy."

A SEAFARING fellow recalls an engineer he sailed with who was a most contemplative cove.

He would enter the Control Room and state: "If things don't change around here soon," (at which point he would pause in a most suspenseful manner) "they will just have to stay the way they are."

ANOTHER of the above chap's profound pronouncements was: "Why are we all here? Because we are not all there."

THE location is the Springburn Caley rail works, where a few of the lads are enjoying a skive behind the smiddy, lounging contentedly in the sun. Quite suddenly a fighter jet swoops across the sky at astonishing speed.

One of the skivers, a wee fellow named Jackie, says: "If you think he's going fast now, just wait till he gets into the countryside."

THERE was once a pilot who entered planes he was booked to fly wearing a trench coat. He then sat down in the rear of the cabin. When the plane door closed for take-off and nothing happened, he would jump out of his seat and storm up the aisle, declaring to the alarm of the passengers: "If nobody's going to fly this thing, I'll do it myself."

COMEDIAN Andy Cameron recalls his mysterious Uncle Joe, who was married to his father's sister.

This curious chap was in the navy, yet somehow managed to make it home every weekend.

"My grandfather referred to him as 'the dry land sailor'," chuckles Andy.

ON his retirement Russell Smith from Largs was "treated" to a jaunt in a two-seater plane. Rather disconcertingly, the pilot turned out to be older than his passenger. After this doddery chap had been assisted into the cockpit, and the plane was in mid-flight, Russell tentatively enquired what would happen if he became unwell at the controls.

"You'd get your name in the papers," was the matter-of-fact response.

THE Campbeltown herring fleet was stormbound at anchor off the Isle of Barra. In one cabin the fishermen passed the time by participating in a spirited game of I Spy.

One worthy fellow had his crewmates perplexed with his contribution of "L L".

When all the competitors had given up in bemused frustration, this chap proudly proclaimed: "Lectric light."

IT was the middle of December and a Glasgow teacher had decided to put up a Christmas tree in her Primary 1 class.

She informed her pupils that if they brought in festive ornamentation for the tree they could spend the day decorating it. The eager children duly arrived with glittering trinkets carefully wrapped in tissue paper. Except for one bold youth who stoutly declared: "Ma faither said you should buy yer ain baubles."

ANOTHER seafaring tale. Ian Craig from Strathaven once overheard a bosun, a McNeil from Barra, say to the newly appointed able seaman: "I never saw you before today, unless, of course, you saw me."

(No doubt the able seaman became unable while attempting to figure out just what the bosun was babbling about.)

ANOTHER mini-epic of the high seas. George Smith from Clydebank tells us a chief engineer he sailed with once gave him the following helpful advice: "Never argue with a woman or a wire rope. Both can prove fatal."

Was the chief engineer being chauvinistic, rope-inistic . . . or both? We really can't decide.

THERE was once a curmudgeonly ship's crew who used their logbook to air personal grievances against fellow shipmates. The skipper recorded in the book that the first mate was: "Drunk again last night."

This did not please the sozzled seafaring chap in question.

So in the following day's ship's log he wrote disapprovingly: "Skipper sober again last night."

A COMELY young wench was discovered after hiding on a vessel for three weeks. She explained to the captain that she was heading for America, and that the first officer had taken her on.

The captain informed her that he certainly had taken her on.

For she was aboard the Renfrew Ferry.

A PILOT was training for his captaincy with BA's exceedingly customer-friendly Highland Division, who are based in Glasgow. His plane was seconds from take-off for Stornoway when Air Traffic Control got in touch to explain that an elderly lady, a Mrs MacLeod, had arrived late at the gate and missed the flight. Would the plane come back for her?

As there were only twenty passengers on board, and half of them probably knew Mrs MacLeod, the decision was taken to taxi back down the runway to pick up the lucky latecomer.

IT is with a fair amount of shame that we repeat the tale of the Clyde steamer captain who, quite possibly, was not a leading light in the feminist movement.

About to depart from the pier at Craigendoran, he spied a late passenger hurrying towards the boat and was heard to grumble: "Ach, why does the last man always have to be a woman?"

A GROUP of seafaring fellows were discussing the most dangerous cargos each of them had sailed with. Crude oil, aviation spirits and naphtha were all nominated. One of the chaps argued that "beans" were the most volatile cargo.

"What kind of beans?" he was asked.

"Human beans," he replied.

SEAFARING yarns – continued. Peter Sommerville from Greenock recalls that during his time at sea first-trippers were told to collect scraps of food to feed the mules, prior to arriving at the Panama Canal.

There was always great disappointment when the naive sailors discovered that the "mules" were in fact small locomotives that pulled the ships through the various locks.

ANOTHER floaty, boaty story. Malcolm Boyd from Milngavie studied to be a ship's engineer at Glasgow's Nautical College. The course combined theory and practical knowledge, meaning students served aboard a ship before taking their written examinations, collectively referred to as the "screen test".

The reason exams were known by this name was because passing them ensured young sailors could triumphantly return to the sea on film-star wages.

(Though, alas, no shiny Oscar was ever handed out. Even to those burly seafaring fellows with more than a passing resemblance to George Clooney . . . or Jennifer Aniston.)

TWO Campbeltown fishing skippers at sea spent an hour inconsiderately discussing golf on the VHF radio channel normally used by the fleet for more serious communication.

The golfing geezers droned on in boring detail about their weekend on the famous Machrihanish course. Clubs used . . . putting technique . . . bunker escapes . . . yadda, yadda, yadda.

When he hauled his gear, one of the golfing chums dolefully reported to his pal that he had netted a huge boulder, weighing several tons, and he had no idea how to get rid of it.

Before the pal could reply, a voice from another vessel boomed over the radio: "Use your f*****g sand wedge."

"THERE'S an old nautical saying that in every port in the world you'll find three things: rats, fleas and Scotsmen," says a reader.

(Though only one of them is likely to know how to deep-fry a Mars Bar, we add with some pride.)

A KIRKINTILLOCH seafarer recalls a trip he took which happened to be the final voyage of the skipper, who was retiring.

On his last night aboard, this old salt allowed the ship's young cadets to almost sink him below the waterline with their many questions. One asked what he remembered of his first voyage.

The misty-eyed mariner said his recollections went so far back that he could recall when Long John Silver still had two legs and carried an egg on his shoulder.

A SAD tale of the traumas of childhood. A little girl in a primary school class was summoned to the headmaster's office to discuss some rather serious events at home. On the youngster's return her teacher anxiously enquired if everything was all right.

"Aye," said the girl. "A' wis playin' wi' ma mammy's teeth last night, an' she wis wonderin' where a' had pit them."

THE Diary's passion for polite, non-prurient language prompts reader Alasdair Sinclair to recall Dunoon Grammar School in the 1960s, which managed to avoid any hint of scholarly impropriety by having inscribed on the staffroom doors: "Masters" and . . . "Lady Teachers".

ANOTHER tale of scholarly impropriety. A reader recalls a high school English lesson in the early 1950s. Asked to give the adjective of apostle, one student, possibly a little less worldly-wise than the others, ventured: "Apostitute."

Cue sniggers all round.

12

Fitba Crazy

ONE thing you can say about our national football team's appearances in major competitions. We never outstay our welcome.

We're not like one of those boorish bores who turn up at a dinner party, drink too much wine, then end up staying the night in a guest bedroom, too tipsy to toddle off home in the car.

Nope. Scotland arrive on time, and leave before the cheese and crackers.

Though perhaps we should try and stick around just a little bit longer. Not by playing better football, of course. That's probably beyond our lads' abilities.

Instead, we should hire expert groveller and former Speaker of the House of Commons, John Bercow, to plead our case to be reinstated whenever we get kicked out of a major competition. A task he'll hopefully undertake with the same amount of ardour he exercised when toadying after a seat in the House of Lords earlier this year. (It didn't work. He's still an icky commoner.)

The Diary is very much like Scotland's footy stars. We don't stick around for long either.

The following sporting yarns are taut, trim and pithy to the point of perfection . . .

RECENT research reveals the universe is 14 billion years old, give or take an hour or two. Russell Smith from Largs is surprised that in all that time Scotland has never won the World Cup. "Is time running out?" he nervously enquires.

ALAN Gordon was a university graduate with the unique distinction of playing for Hearts, Hibs, Dundee and Dundee United. When he was at Hibs, manager Eddie Turnbull was outlining a tactic he wanted to adopt. Alan interrupted and suggested an amendment to the instructions.

Turnbull glowered at him, then said: "The trouble with you, son, is that all your brains are in your head."

FOOTY broadcaster Jim Spence believes Aberdeen made the right choice in agreeing a deal for striker Fraser Hornby.

"Good to see the Dons have signed Hornby," says Jim. "That'll get them back on track. It'll be full steam ahead now."

BACK in February, Scotland managed to beat England in a footy match. Patriotic Scots language poet Len Pennie (also known as Miss PunnyPennie) explained how best to describe this stirring victory using traditional phraseology.

Apparently the most appropriate thing to say is: "Git it wrapped right roond yous."

NOT many Celtic fans were disappointed when Neil Lennon resigned as manager, though he still has a few supporters, including comedian Mark Nelson, who says: "It is important to remember all the great things Neil Lennon did. For Rangers, Ross County, Sparta Prague . . ."

THERE has been some positive activity on the pitch for Celtic, with David Turnbull proving to be one of Scotland's most promising young players. According to Football

Wonderkids, a website monitoring the statistics of up-and-coming players, Turnbull made more key passes in the 20/21 season than any other youngster in Europe.

The Diary concludes that the only footy star to challenge Turnbull in this area would be Frank McAvennie in his pomp.

Though, of course, most of Frank's passes weren't made on the pitch . . .

RANGERS win the 2020/21 league and receive congratulations from former Celtic player Chris Sutton. Though we're not sure he's being entirely sincere when he says on social media: "Well done to Steven Gerrard and Rangers on a brilliant season, and one in a row."

RESPONDING indignantly to the above story, reader Charlie Robertson (who we surmise may own one or two T-shirts of the true blue hue) says: "Just wait till the Gers win a hundred in a row. I bet Chris Sutton won't be sniggering then."

A NUMBER of Rangers fans celebrated their historic league win while not adhering to social-distancing diktats.

Reader Hugh Dougherty suggests a new song should be added to the club's songbook to encourage the miscreants to reflect on the error of their ways . . . 'The Mask My Father Wore'.

A BISHOPBRIGGS Bhoy got rather excited after erroneously assuming that former Bournemouth boss Eddie Howe was about to take over at Celtic. He told us he was looking forward to the new manager being lauded with newspaper headlines such as: "Why Howe?", "Howe No?" and "Howe, Will This Work Out?"

IT was the news that shook the footballing world to its foundations. Six of the UK's top teams agreed to join a new European Super League. The names involved were glorious and gold-drenched. Manchester City! Man United! Chelsea! Liverpool! Arsenal! Tottenham Hotspur!

But one proud team refused to join the jubilant jamboree.

Glasgow's Maryhill Football Club. (Who play in the West of Scotland Football League.)

"Maryhill FC will not be joining the European Super League," the team revealed in a statement to the world, before explaining the background to the brave decision.

"We haven't been asked," they admitted.

THE emergence of the European Super League was rapidly followed by its disintegration. This, in turn, resulted in some curious knock-on effects.

"My wife and dog have announced a breakaway super household," revealed Glasgow-based actor and comedian Johnny Mac, who added despondently: "I didn't make the top six . . . and there are only three of us in the house."

MANCHESTER City reached the Champions League final in 2021. Everybody in Scotland was delighted for the English team, with our generous footy fans showing no sense of grievance at a lack of tartan talent in the top echelons of the game.

Dundonian sports broadcaster Jim Spence underlined how grudge-free our nation is when he said of Man City's impressive achievement: "It's an inspiration for every club with only a few billion to spend."

IN the month of May chaos ensues at Old Trafford when local footy fans protest by invading the pitch. A Diary reader says: "The actions of a few hundred Man United fans ruined the match for the 700 million proper supporters in Asia."

THERE'S an Italian footballer called Kevin Lasagna, we are reliably informed by a reader, who adds: "Apparently he's a man of many layers who doesn't mince his words."

IN the 1950s there was a radio broadcast of a Scotland–England international. Scottish defender Sammy Cox suffered a bad injury early on and didn't reappear for the second half. In those days no substitutes were allowed. So when the teams came out for the final forty-five minutes the radio broadcaster announced: "Here come ten brave Scots without Cox."

A HEATED debate takes place in school common rooms across the nation. For once, the dispute isn't about whether chemistry teachers should be allowed to concoct frothing liquid compounds that, when swallowed, help them to beat the fitter and faster PE teachers in a beanbag race to the death.

Instead, the discussion centres on whether pupils should be allowed to watch the Scotland footy team play in the Euros during school hours.

A teacher from Glasgow's Southside discusses the matter with colleagues. They conclude that the youngsters can indulge in some patriotic gogglebox ogling.

The teacher tells us: "We also decided that if Scotland lose there will be punishment exercises all round. That should ensure the cheers for the home nation are extra rapturous."

ALAS, Scotland do lose their first game in the Euros, against the Czech Republic. The nation is despondent, apart from linguistically limber Norman McAllister from Hamilton.

Rubbing salt in a very nippy wound, he says of the result: "After their victory, the Czechs were fairly bouncing."

GLASGOW singer Amy Macdonald also manages to be optimistic about Scotland's defeat by revealing she is glad many kids were allowed to watch the game at school.

"This is the sort of crushing disappointment that sets you up for life," she says, approvingly.

DURING a Euros press conference, footballing icon Ronaldo appears to snub fizzy drink company Coca-Cola by pushing away their beverage and holding aloft a bottle of water. Bert Buchan wants Scotland captain Andy Robertson to do something similar at future press conferences. "Only instead of that hideous H_2O stuff he should triumphantly raise a bottle of Irn-Bru," says our reader.

THE odious organisers of the Euros devise a cruel and unusual punishment for the Tartan Army following Scotland's initial defeat.

They force our chaps to play two more games.

Reader Darren Edwards explains why he won't be watching either fixture. "If I want disappointment in my life, it's just as easy to tune into Nicola Sturgeon's latest update about lockdown easing."

SCOTLAND play England at Wembley in the Euros and manage to eke out a draw. English crime writer Christopher Fowler admits to being rather startled by the visiting fans from faraway, fabled Alba.

He sends out a distressed report, revealing that the London underground is "filled with hundreds of drunk, unintelligible, maskless fat men in little pleated skirts".

The rather confused novelist adds: "I think they may be Norwegians or something."

GLASGOW broadcaster Paul Coia and his English wife Debbie watch Scotland play England in the Euros. Debbie's verdict on the match shows her astute knowledge of the beautiful game: "The blue strip is nicer," she says. "It's more slimming."

THE trauma of watching our national footy team fumble, flail and flop is over for another year. Scotland lose their third match against Croatia and are out the competition.

Reader Julie McAlpine describes the situation best: "Watching Scotland and believing we can win is like a second marriage. A triumph of hope against experience."

FOR some inexplicable reason the Euros aren't cancelled, even though Scotland are no longer taking part and the entire enterprise now seems rather pointless.

Stranger still, some people continue to watch the remaining matches on telly.

Two such eccentric individuals are Gavin Horgan and his thirteen-year-old son, John, who watched Portugal play France.

At one point John said approvingly of the action: "That was an audacious chip!"

Impressed, Dad said: "Your vocabulary's improving."

"It's no biggy," shrugged the youngster. "I've been using the word chip for ages."

READER John Fallon is grumpy and unforgiving about Scotland's Euro exit and believes 'Yes Sir, I Can Boogie' should no longer be our nation's unofficial anthem.

He now hopes an enterprising singer will release a song titled: 'Yes Sir, I'm Still Fine With the Boogying. It's the Kicking the Ball Around a Park That Needs a Lot of Work.'

THE above story reminds reader Eric Macdonald of the team who entered a golf tournament and chose to play under the rather uninspiring name: 'Yes Sir, I Can Bogey.'

THE Scots finally celebrate a palpable triumph at the Euros.

Former Rangers striker Ally McCoist takes up a commentary role with ITV and immediately impresses viewers from all across the UK with his golden-tongued gab.

At one point he even manages to sneakily slip the Scottish word "outwith" onto network TV.

A stunning strike for the crafty centre-forward.

CYNICS may claim that our nation's footy fans take more delight in an English loss than a Scottish victory. Not true.

We may have had a few insignificant skirmishes with our southern neighbours in the past, but the Diary is proud to proclaim that, in these enlightened times, the generous and decent folk of Alba shared the Anglo Saxon rabble's giddy pleasure when they triumphed over Germany at Wembley in the Euros.

Ed Miller from Cumbernauld puts it best, when he says: "Having something new to celebrate will hopefully stop the English banging on about '66 for at least ten minutes."

ENGLAND also defeat the doughty Danes, continuing an impressive run of Euro wins. Many English fans can't stop themselves from chanting: "Football's coming home . . ."

"Not unless it's heading to China," responds reader Calvin Black. "The rules of the game were introduced there, back in 216 BCE."

Calvin adds: "The English didn't invent chopsticks either. Though Baddiel and Skinner have probably composed a song that says they did."

AT last. The final game of the Euros, and it's between those brave, charming and pretty darn wonderful Italians and some other blokes. (Oh, yes. It's the English. And they lose.)

Reader Lindsay Young remains exasperated about an earlier match where Raheem Sterling dramatically tumbled over in the box, with seemingly little provocation, and grabbed a penalty for England.

"The Queen will have to cancel a knighthood for Raheem," predicts Lindsay. "She'll be worried that tapping his shoulder with a sword could lead to an attempted murder charge."

WE haven't quite exhausted the topic of the Euros. Australia-based Scottish comedian Dave Callan tells us that the rather skewed BBC-style commentary that invariably favours the English team, while downplaying other nations' chances, has now infected antipodean sports broadcasting.

One of the Aussie TV channels hired an English bloke to pontificate about footy. This chap proudly proclaimed that he had picked Italy as his "dark horse" team to win the Euros.

That would be the same "dark horse" Italy who have won four World Cups and remain unbeaten since 2018.

13

A Grand Place to Have a Near-Fatal Accident

LONG-TERM readers of our column may wonder why the Diary doesn't have its own prize-giving ceremony for those who send us stories. The answer is, of course, that appearing in the Diary is reward enough. It's such an illustrious achievement that it may eventually make its way onto the headstones of many of our contributors.

Carved in marble will be the words: "Here lies so-and-so. Proud mother (or father) to two lovely children. Captain of industry. Leader of nations. Loved by many. Admired by all. And – most importantly – the originator of a crackpot comment that was once published in The Herald Diary."

Surely nothing is more gratifying than appearing in our daily newspaper column? Well, surprisingly, something is.

Appearing in our annual Diary Book.

Which is exactly what the following contributors all manage to achieve, this very instant, as they smuggle themselves into the following chapter . . .

CURIOUS goings-on at Glasgow Uni. Gilbert MacKay from Newton Mearns recalls a university psychology class where one of his fellow students was called Fred, while two of the lecturers were named Dr Huggin and Dr McKissack.

Meaning that sometimes it was possible to witness (though never in the back seat) Huggin and McKissack with Fred.

A READER alerts us to a memory of being taught by a Dr Shirley, who once memorably explained a point about statistics with the aid of three knitting needles and a potato.

THERE was a Glasgow University lecturer whose special interest was Greek mythology. He owned two dogs: one named Psyche (after a hound that featured in *A Life of Bliss*, a popular radio programme) and the other was Achilles.

When the lecturer took the second of these mutts for a walk, he could often be heard shouting: "Achilles . . . heel!"

THREE ladies were on a bus tour of the Highlands and found themselves on the CalMac ferry from Oban to Craignure. The boat departed and the group were informed that the shop was now open. Off they rushed to purchase . . . duty-free goods.

They returned, much deflated, grumbling that they were astonished not to find any cheap booze, unlike the ferry they'd taken to France where there were duty-free bargains galore.

A CHUM of a Kilmarnock reader was suffering from a sore eye, but couldn't get a surgery appointment. Instead, a medical official told him to get his wife to photograph the irritated orb and email the image to the doctor. "I bet she was glad the problem wasn't piles," says our reader.

OUR readers are a vigorous bunch, but sometimes they are confronted by information that forces them to be aware of the fatal finger of Father Time tap-tapping on their shoulders.

A friend of Brian Johnston from Torrance informed him that the release date of The Beatles album *Abbey Road* is closer to the First World War than it is to the year 2021.

Did that make our correspondent feel old?

"Order me a stairlift and pass the Sanatogen," he shudders.

A SOUTH Ayrshire reader going by the name of Auld Sanny admits that the future of motoring has him worried.

"What should you do when your computerised self-driving car mows down a pedestrian?" he asks. "Do you just switch it off, switch it back on again, and continue on your way?"

It's a tricky situation. Though having jumped into our time machine and taken a jaunt into the future to pick up the updated version of the *Highway Code*, the Diary is delighted to confirm the correct protocol.

You should phone for a computer-controlled ambulance which will arrive on the scene with a mechanical medic in the back, who will then conclude that the pedestrian you bumped into was actually a robot, whose life can be saved by the addition of petrol plus a washer or two.

The future ... it's a grand place to have a near-fatal accident.

MULLING over the above story, a reader adds that in such a utopia/dystopia (take your pick) people will no longer need to phone for medical assistance.

Instead, they will send a text with a symbol specifically devised for summoning an ambulance in an emojincy.

"JAMES Bond always does amazing feats in restrictive tailored suits," points out reader Tony Miller. "Imagine what he could accomplish in tracky bottoms and a string vest."

A DIARY tale about playing I Spy reminds reader John Nisbet of the time a maintenance crew at a manufacturing firm in Ayr played the same game during their break. One chap said he spied an object with the initials I and P. After many failed guesses the other participants conceded.

They were informed that the answer was an: "iil poorie". Or to translate from the colloquial into English . . . an oil can.

Our reader is unsure if this answer was accepted by the other contestants with good grace.

He suspects not.

REFERRING to the above tale, Edith McInroy from Kilwinning says her father and his pals used the "iil poorie" term for a curlew, a bird common in the countryside where they lived.

So it's either an oil can . . . or a feathered beaky thing.

The Scots language is turning out to be a tricky trapdoor which descends into darkness and obscurity. Is it any wonder that our nation still hasn't won the I Spy World Cup?

WE are told of a hopefully apocryphal tale about several unexpected deaths in the same hospital bed during the 1990s. After a lengthy investigation it transpired that a cleaner had been switching off the life support machine every Friday to plug in the floor polisher.

Was anybody charged with negligence, we wonder. Or did the culprit make a clean getaway?

WATCHING a BBC news report, Doug Maughan spotted a barbershop in the background with the wonderfully appropriate name "Ali Barber".

WHEN Jane Marshall told her seven-year-old daughter her mobile phone was in airplane mode, the youngster replied: "So can it fly?"

A COMPASSIONATE thought from reader Darren Edwards: "There are probably loads of unlucky vampires who have been hit by cars that were backing up because the driver couldn't see anybody in the rear-view mirror."

RELAXING in a beer garden recently, Geoff Crowley overheard two chaps in their twenties discussing romance.

Said one chap to the other, "I've met this girl called Natasha and she wants me to call her Tash."

"So what's the problem?" enquired his chum.

Gesturing to the resplendently fuzzy area under his own nose, the first chap said: "I've already got a 'tash. I'm not sure I need two in my life."

A CELEBRITY tale in this book revolved around the fact that in Glasgow Hank Marvin means both a pop star from the 1960s and a rumbling belly from any era.

Fraser Kelly tells us that in the Philippines, the phrase for being hungry is linked to another '60s star . . . Tom Jones.

Our reader is unsure how such strange terminology came into being.

"But in my neck of the woods," he adds, "it's not unusual."

"THERE should be an award for the most sceptical person in the UK," claims a reader, who adds: "Though the most sceptical person in the UK would probably find a very good reason to turn down such an award."

THE Diary was sad to hear of the threatened closure of the McVitie's biscuit factory in Tollcross. We recall an anecdote told by a lady who worked there.

Reminiscing about her time on the shop floor, this former employee said: "The woman in charge of the recipe room I worked in was called Vera Love. She was so proper and lady-like that if you needed to go to the toilet you weren't allowed to use the word 'toilet' and you certainly didn't say bog or cludgie or kazi. You had to call it the 'bathroom'."

HAIRDRESSING salons and a certain book are the two main culprits when it comes to inflicting excruciating puns on an aggrieved public. The book in question is of course the one you hold in your hands. You may have noticed that we referred to a snippety-snip joint called Ali Barber a few stories ago.

A reader adds to the pun-ishment by telling us: "When I grow up, I'm going to have a barber salon that I'll call The Royal Hair Force."

THINKING about big business, reader Stephen Campbell says: "There must be some teenagers who have grown up believing Jeff Bezos bought a rainforest and named it after his company."

WEARING his Covid mask in the local pharmacy, Malcolm Boyd from Milngavie said to the person at the counter: "The repeat prescription for Malcolm Boyd . . . or The Lone Ranger."

The pharmacist, a good sport, replied: "Where does the Lone Ranger live?"

Malcolm confirmed his address and the lady handed over the prescription, dryly adding: "Hi Ho Silver, away."

SIGNS are useful. They instruct us how to behave and prevent us becoming unnecessarily reckless by improvising our lives as we go along. Case in point. Reader Beryl Parker came across a sign on a door that read: "Please open door before entering."

Beryl was grateful for the advice. "I was seconds away from attempting to charge head first through the door while it was still closed," she says.

OVERHEARD in a Glasgow nightclub . . .

Girl 1: Wit d'ye hink o' ma new shoes?

Girl 2: (giving shoes an intense, critical perusal) If them heels were oany higher, the drug squad wid be efter 'em.

A CHUBBY chum of reader Sarah Sutherland was frustrated because she couldn't fit into a favourite dress.

Attempting to encourage her pal to diet, Sarah said: "Remember, you are what you eat."

"Oh goody," said her chum. "In that case I'm going to eat a thin person."

MAKING a complete spectacle of herself, reader Claire Lane says: "When I put on my glasses my nose and ears do all the heavy lifting while my eyes get all the benefit. It hardly seems fair, somehow."

THE twelve-year-old son of reader Melony Portis is a thoughtful chap. Gazing out the window on a dreich day, he muttered: "I wish the world was a Pot Noodle."

His mother asked why. The youngster pointed to the rain dashing the window.

"A Pot Noodle improves when you add water," he explained.

THE mother of Charles Perry from Ayr is a film buff who knows loads about movie stars. Though how she judges their performances can be eccentric.

Watching a classic Cary Grant movie at home, she said: "Isn't Cary talented? He's never looked at the camera once."

THE charity behind Cornwall's famous "indoor rainforest", the Eden Project, is planning to build a similarly impressive greenhouse in an old gasworks in Dundee.

A reader says: "Wouldn't it be nice if they could make the roof out of old jeelly jars? Or better still, visitors could be welcomed by the strains of a new version of 'Hey Jute'. I'm sure Paul McCartney would be up for it."

STUDYING English at the University of Glasgow, reader Lisa Murphy happened to be lounging on the couch in her student flat, reading *Sense and Sensibility*. Her flatmate glanced over and said: "That looks interesting. Is it a sequel to *Dumb and Dumber?*"

"I've always wondered if he was joking," says Lisa. "But as he was studying engineering, my suspicion is that he was deadly serious."

VISITING Whitstable in Kent, a reader spotted a shellfish restaurant. Nearby was a venue that was suspiciously named the Oyster Indoor Bowling Centre.

"I'm offended," snorts our reader. "It suggests an imposition of unnecessary cruelty on molluscs. Imagine bowling with oysters. Can't folk in Whitstable use those large, heavy balls like the rest of us?"

MUSICAL musings from reader Claire Lane, who says: "Headphones are audio drinking straws for those who prefer Mozart to Milkshakes."

OVERHEARD on a train . . .

Passenger 1: Did you watch the nature programme last night?

Passenger 2: Aye. A didnae like they Quasimodo dragons with their forked tongues. They gave me the hump.

FINDING himself without scissors in the house, Harvey Graham bought a pair from the shops. At home he discovered the scissors were sealed inside a bag it was impossible to tear open.

"If only I had scissors then I could cut the bag open," Harvey mused to himself. Then he realised he did indeed have scissors. Inside the bag. Which he couldn't open without the aid of scissors.

"I felt like a physicist trying to comprehend the origins of the universe," our reader explains. "Once things get going everything makes sense. But how does the Big Bang start in the first place?"

THE twentieth wedding anniversary of Carol Taylor didn't go as hoped. "My husband and I had dinner I prepared, then I washed the dishes," says Carol. Glancing at her chafed hands in the soap suds, our reader sighed.

"What started out as marital bliss quickly turned into marital blisters," she says.

PRINCE William and Kate Middleton became bingo callers during a virtual visit to a nursing home. Reader Scott Fowler believes the Royal pair should have adapted the traditional bingo "call-outs" into something more regal.

He suggests "Cup of tea, number three" could be: "Footman grovelling on bended knee, number three."

THE Diary receives some curious notifications. Researchers get in touch to inform us that they have discovered which male and female names are most likely to end up with a criminal conviction.

They claim that chaps called David and Daniel, or ladies named Sarah and Amy, have the greatest probability of a dalliance with the law.

We remain unpersuaded. Surely the only crime a Daniel or an Amy will ever be found guilty of is a felony against highfalutin fashion if they turn up at Ascot wearing last year's cravat or summer hat?

Meanwhile, we have devised an alternative, and far more accurate, list of criminal monikers.

And top of our pile?

The names Mugsy, Knuckles and Snake-Eye Lil, of course.

WE continue devising alternative number call-outs for William and Kate to try. Mick Doyle suggests: "Fifty-four. Of Harry and Meghan, we don't wanna hear more."

SOME children have very grand names, a reader points out. In a Byres Road supermarket he heard a Glesga wifie call her grandson to heel with the words: "Salvador! Salvador!"

"I wonder if his surname was Daily?" muses our reader.

ANOTHER bingo call-out rhyme for Prince William or Kate to try. Tod Bruce from Paisley suggests that when calling the number fifty-nine, William should yell: "Fifty-nine – if only it wasn't Papa who was First in Line."

POLITICAL aide Dominic Cummings is in the news an awful lot. He's now so famous he'll probably start wearing a long black wig and calling himself Kardashian Sister Number Four.

Bombarded with relentless information about Boris's former helper, reader Albert Kavanagh turned to his wife and said: "What d'you think of Dominic Cummings?"

Albert's wife, who is a little hard of hearing, answered: "A Domino's pizza's coming? I didn't even know we'd ordered."

"I MANAGED to burn three thousand calories," boasts reader Martina Kay. With slightly less bombast, she adds: "That's the last time I leave brownies in the oven while I'm having a snooze."

VISITING an Inchinnan bowling club, reader Jim Morrison overhears the following conversation:

"Willie, d'ye have trouble deciding which is the back and which is the front when you're pulling on a plain-coloured crew-neck jumper? Because I do."

"Not at all," responds Willie. "The front's usually got stains oan it."

RETIRED Labour MP Sir Brian Donohoe recalls being on an employment panel for a bus driver who had inspected his vehicle at the end of a shift and discovered an intriguing parcel. Instead of delivering it to lost property he unwrapped it and discovered a white stick with a pair of dark glasses.

For some reason he decided to wear the glasses and carry the cane when he arrived for his next shift. He then asked a wee wuman to guide him to his bus where he jumped into the driver's seat and drove off with his horrified passengers screaming in terror.

Brian tells us the sympathetic employment panel let the rogue roadster off with a final warning.

Thus proving that justice truly is blind.

BROWSING an ancient magazine discovered in a loft, exhausted mother of two, Lauren Evans, noticed an article with the headline "Problems That Arise When Hiring a Fulltime Nanny".

"That's a problem I'd gladly accept," says Lauren. "It's like someone whinging that their back is killing them because they've got too many gold coins stuffed in their rucksack."

GLASGOW Uni is world famous for its bright spark under-graduates. Reader Iain MacLean recalls visiting the student union and spotting graffiti which proudly proclaimed: "I always wanted to be an engineer and now I are one."

A CHUM of Rory Hartley happened to mention he was glad the pubs were opening again as he had missed the yummy soup which his favourite hostelry regularly served him.

"And what soup is that?" asked our reader.

"Whisky with ice croutons," replied his chum.

THE Diary is in awe of students and their learned ways, which is why we continue to celebrate the profound scribblings on the toilet doors of the University of Glasgow Union.

A reader recalls one especially beautiful rhyming couplet:

"It's no use standing on the seat

The spirochaete can jump six feet."

(Spirochaete is a type of bacteria, we feel duty bound to add. Though we are scientifically unqualified to say whether it can jump six feet, even on a good day. Perhaps it has a chance, if it happens to be training for the high-jump in the Bacteria Olympics . . .)

SUPERMARKETS that do deliveries are a welcome addition to modern life. Though the practice has a downside. Rebecca Bowles gets her groceries dispatched to her house and knows the routine well.

1) Thrilled to hear a knock on the door. Yay! The goodies have arrived!

2) Empty bags. Horrified to discover half the stuff ordered isn't there. And the stuff that *has* been sent isn't what was ordered.

3) Spend the week bitterly eating food you hate and wouldn't thrust on your worst enemy.

4) Make another order. And cross fingers . . .

"Getting my shopping has become like life in general," says Rebecca. "You dream. Your dreams are dashed. You dare to dream again."

ANOTHER tale of garrulous graffiti. Attending a BT training school, a reader once spotted on a toilet door the message: "Don't beam me up yet, Scotty, I'm just about tooooooo . . ."

The final run of o's stretched all the way to the top of the door.

STROLLING down Buchanan Street with his wife, reader James Conway spotted a teenager wearing a pair of jeans which were slashed and shredded in the fashionable style.

"I bet they cost a lot of money," James whispered to his wife.

"Yes," she replied. "A rip-off in more ways than one."

HOUSEPROUD reader Gemma Young was having a discussion with her husband about updating the decor in the couple's bedroom.

Hubby was rather less than enthusiastic about the idea,

and grumped: "Why should we spend money on a room where we're unconscious ninety-five per cent of the time?"

ANOTHER tale of villainous vandalism. In the 1970s Strathclyde Uni attempted to eradicate a plague of graffiti by redecorating the toilet walls in the Reading Room with a closely stippled surface similar to Artex.

While it encouraged the use of shorter sentences, it made little difference to the quantity of reading material on offer. One such contribution read: "How do you b******s find flat bits to write on?" It was signed: "The Jannie."

OUR readers like to tell us how difficult their early years were, when everything was in short supply and the only joy of childhood was provided by the flickering hope of one day growing up to be a noble and justly celebrated contributor to the Herald Diary.

In this frame of mind, Lionel Collins gets in touch to say: "As a kid I was so poor that for breakfast I had no choice but to eat Ordinary K."

WE have a fondness for businesses that trade under clever monikers. In Castelculier, a village just south of the rugby capital Agen, there is a hairdresser called Hair du Temps.

L'air du temps – as those with a French/English dictionary at hand will know – means: "The spirit of the age" or "The current trend".

Clearly Gallic snippety-snip merchants adore a pun as much as their British counterparts.

WE continue discussing the scholarly scribbles scrawled on toilet doors. A reader once competed in a sports event in Fraserburgh where so many men's teams were taking part that some of the blokes had to use the women's dressing area, where the graffiti was of a much higher order than the literary output usually found in a chaps' changing room.

It included the following pithy and poetical masterpiece:
"A girl's ambition must be small,
To write his name upon this wall."

NOSTALGIC Stewart Daniels from Fife reminisces about a more innocent era. "If the world really is improving as some people believe," he says, "how come I can recall when Zoom was an ice lolly you bought for 6d and it didn't mean struggling not to snooze through a conference call with your boss?"

A SHERLOCK Holmes joke in the Diary rouses a reader to puff on his meerschaum pipe, put on his deerstalker cap and head into the smog-smothered streets, investigating the possibilities of discovering an equally funny gag. And, by Jove, he's found one.

Dr Watson is horrified to discover Holmes has changed the colour of his front door.

"Holmes! Why did you paint your door that hideous shade

of yellow?" says the great detective's friend.

Holmes responds: "Lemon entry, my dear Watson."

MORE toilet humour. Reader John Hart recalls a pay-to-use lavatory in Glasgow city centre with a space beneath the door, next to which someone had scribbled: "Please close this gap. The Limbo Dancers are getting in for free."

MODERN communication has a downside, as reader Brian Chrystal discovered. Attempting to text his daughter, his phone's autocorrect decided it had a better idea what Brian wanted to say than he did himself. It kept changing toerags to storage.

"Not quite the same nuance in Glasgow," says our reader. "See youse, ya wee storage lockers . . ."

FLUSHED with zeal to raise the cultural level of the Diary's run of toilet tales, Alasdair Sinclair recalls the words he discovered on the flyleaf of a second-hand Latin dictionary:

Lines Written in an Oxford Bog

"O Cloacina, goddess of this place
And votary of every man of grace,
Safe to thy throne may our oblations flow –"
Not rudely swift, nor obstinately slow."

TOILET humour again. In the 60s, youth hostel lavatory doors were often daubed with the message: "Kilroy was here."

Glen Nevis hostel was an exception, recalls a reader. The notification on that particular door was:
  "I leap in mirth and jump for joy,
  "For I was here before Kilroy."

WE continue recalling the picaresque pictorial adventures of a gent called Kilroy.

Richard Davis, who is based in Vienna, believes there should be an updated equivalent of Kilroy to reflect the impositions placed on public activity over the last year and a bit.

He suggests: "Killjoy was here."

FURTHER celebrations of graffiti with added gravitas. Reader Craig McCall has been pondering a politically astute example of the artform he recently spotted scrawled on a wall, which read: "Is Karl Marx's grave a communist plot?"

PICTURE this. A reader recalls the miniscule writing that was once scrawled on the inside base of a toilet door in Glasgow University Union, which helpfully read: "For goodness sake, sit back."

SATISFIED Stewart Daniels from Cairneyhill admits that he's been enjoying our focus on all things graffiti, though he fears it will be short-lived.

"Graffiti is dead," he informs us. "The writing's on the wall."

14

A Hirsute Hound Named Percy

WHEN Joe Biden met Boris Johnson in Cornwall for the G7 meeting, the American President presented his British counterpart with a gift of a bicycle and helmet. The addition of the helmet was a nice touch. A not-so-subtle dig at Boris's bumpy brand of leadership, which often involves colliding with uncomfortable facts, crashing through protocol and riding roughshod over pesky details.

Compared to Boris, a bull in a china shop comes across as a relatively well-behaved customer, deserving of a Loyalty Card at the very least.

BoJo's shortcomings are undeniable, though the Diary must admit to having a soft spot for our glorious leader. For, as the following chapter shows, life's greatest bumblers and stumblers may be a hazard unto themselves and others.

But they can also be pretty darned entertaining . . .

WE hear of an elderly lady who adopts a rescue bulldog, which she names Caesar. During the Holyrood elections, a canvasser arrives at her front door. As the canvasser is leaving, the bulldog decides to race after her.

The old lady shouts: "Caesar! Caesar!"

The dog, never one to ignore a direct order, promptly grabs the canvasser by her ankle.

We assume the dog's name has now been changed to "Here boy".

AS every baffled schoolchild will tell you, the English language is a sneaky trickster that likes to confuse and abuse those who attempt to learn its arcane ways.

Case in point . . . "When you transport something by car, it's called a shipment," says a reader. "But when you transport something by ship, it's called cargo."

IN the month of June a sliver of determined sunshine manages to insert itself between the usual onslaught of Scottish raindrops, much as a svelte chap may attempt to squeeze himself into a packed lift that is bulging with portly passengers.

Many of our readers delight in the dazzle. Though not Stephen Brownlie, the proud owner of a hirsute hound named Percy.

Stephen informs us that his dog suffers greatly in the sunshine. This sad fact inspired our reader to devise a revolutionary invention which he proudly calls the dogasol.

"It's a parasol for pooches," he reveals. "All you have to do is attach a standard parasol to a leash, then your dog can enjoy the shade during walkies."

There are other benefits, too. "A dogasol adds some added elegance to even the scruffiest of mutts," explains Stephen, "turning your pet into a barking boulevardier."

THE weather in Scotland continues its Mr Nice Guy routine. Instead of wind, rain, hail, sleet and snow for seven days in a row, there is only wind, rain, hail, sleet and snow for six days in a row.

Thinking about our intemperate temperature, Ian Noble from Carstairs Village wonders if the citizens of the Baltic states of Latvia, Lithuania or Estonia ever mutter on a cold night: "It's Scottish out there."

SCOTLAND has always been ahead of its time. We are reliably informed by a reader that when the royal navy developed its base on Hoy during the Second World War they built their radio communications centre on a nearby hill which just happened to be called . . . Wee Fea.

"ALLOW food to rest for one minute before eating," must be the most ignored instruction among microwave users," claims reader Andrew McDonnell. "It really should read: 'Allow food to rest for as long as it takes to rip off cellophane and start chomping.'"

THE Diary's 'What the Heckety-Heck is Going On Around Here?' Department (one of the busiest, most overworked divisions in our bureau) has received a message from Alastair Sillars from Dumfries, who informs us that he spotted a sign which read: SECRET BUNKER.

"How can it be secret if it's signposted?" enquires our baffled correspondent.

WE would normally conclude that the following tale from reader Robin Gilmour was a rather unlikely one, though in the current climate it has more than a hint of truth about it. Robin tells us that he spotted a wee old wumman staggering out of the supermarket carrying eight bags of messages and a twenty-four pack of water.

"Can you manage?" enquired our gallant correspondent.

"Aye, son," replied the elderly lady. "But I'm no' wantin' the Celtic job."

BEFORE the days of the CalMac roll-on/roll-off ferry, vehicles had to be craned aboard. One vessel's cargo manifest included the shipment to the Hebrides of a small Bedford bus. The mate calculated that its weight would exceed the derrick's safe working limit.

To solve the problem, a bright deckie suggested removing the wheels of the bus to make the vehicle light enough to lift. This was accomplished, and when the ferry was underway the mate enquired as to the whereabouts of the wheels.

"Och, it was just as handy to put them inside the bus," he was told.

A TALE of undergraduates and their uni-que take on life.

Bryce Drummond from Kilmarnock tells us that when his son was studying architecture at the University of Strathclyde, he claimed that he could invariably tell when an engineering student had been using a computer.

The giveaway? The screen always had Tipp-Ex patches on it.

BBC 4 is broadcasting repeats of the classic drama *Elizabeth R*, first televised fifty years ago.

The six-part series follows the trials and travails of the Tudor monarch Elizabeth the First of England, played by a young Glenda Jackson. At various times in her life she is imprisoned, lied to, betrayed in love and plotted against by the monarchs of France, Spain and even her own courtiers.

Reader Maureen Clarke's enjoyment of the show was interrupted when her husband turned to her and said: "You think Elizabeth is having a rough time now? Wait till Oprah turns up."

STIRLING University professor Christine Ferguson is feeling fulfilled. "Finally," she sighs. "After decades in academia, I am able to include in my syllabus the one thing that is one hundred per cent responsible for both my entire career as a scholar and adult romantic choices: *Carry On Screaming*."

A VIGNETTE of cosmopolitan Glasgow life. A reader was leaving Tesco in Sauchiehall Street when she became aware of a slightly dubious member of the public shouting at the two security guards on the door who were refusing him entry to the shop.

Clearly exasperated by this indignity, the chap appealed to them: "Do I *look* like trouble? Apart from the fact that I've got nae teeth?"

THINKING about how tradesmen advertise their services, David Russell from Penicuik wonders: "Do Grate Builders and Monumental Masons learn their skills at the same school of masonic hyperbole?"

[173]

BUSINESS news. Reader David Donaldson notes that Terry Boot has replaced Peter Foot as financial head of Shoe Zone.

"This takes normative determinism to new heights," says David. "Or lows, depending on how you look at it."

A SUNDAY school teacher asked his class to draw a picture representing the Easter story. Taken by surprise by one little lad's picture of an aeroplane, the teacher enquired about its significance.

The little lad replied: "People are flying off on their Easter holidays, and there's Pontius the pilot."

15

Enter . . . The Nemesis

**THERE have been many epic grudge matches through-
out history.**

Celtic versus Rangers. Muhammad Ali skipping round
George Foreman in the boxing ring. Donald Trump going toe-
to-toe against everyone on Twitter who isn't Donald Trump.

But none of these slam-bam squabbles compares to a certain battle of the giants that took place roughly forty years
ago in a leafy suburb of a Scottish town.

That was where a small boy with curly blond hair and
wide beseeching eyes (imagine Oliver Twist, though cuter,
far cuter) took on an older athlete in a tennis match to the
death. Okay, not quite "to the death", though it did last until
teatime.

That small boy was me. (The hair's no longer blond and
curly, though I'm still adorable.) And the older athlete? It
was my mother, Linda Jackson.

After much pestering, she had agreed to play me a game of tennis in the road outside our terrace house. We didn't have a net. Or professional equipment. Just toy rackets with strings as taut as tadpole nets.

Also, since we were playing on the road, we had to duck and dodge a succession of cars zooming down the middle of Centre Court. This distracting element to the match was undoubtedly the reason I eventually lost, even though I was clearly the more elegant, dynamic and just plain talented athlete.

Since then I've lost various contests to Mum. (Or the Nemesis, as I now think of her.) Games of Ludo. Snakes & Ladders. Monopoly.

The Nemesis doesn't win these trials of strength and aptitude because she's a better sportsperson, of course. She wins because, during that fateful tennis match, she managed to burrow inside my head, and she's been rattling my rhythm and messing with my finely tuned equilibrium ever since.

And the more she wins, the more I hunger for sweet, sweet revenge.

Which explains why I happen to be brandishing a putting iron in Glasgow city centre, steeling myself for a winner-takes-all game of mini-golf.

"Ooh, this'll be fun, won't it?" says the Nemesis, doing her oh-so-typical impersonation of a kindly, five-foot-one retired bank clerk from the Southside of Glasgow.

But I know her wily tricks of old.

"No talking on the field of combat," I growl, marching to the first hole.

At this point I should probably describe the layout of our gladiatorial arena, Jungle Rumble Adventure Golf on Bath Street.

It looks sort of like the Old Course at St Andrews . . . if the Old Course at St Andrews looked nothing like the Old Course at St Andrews.

For instance, St Andrews has rolling fields of verdant splendour. Jungle Rumble doesn't have anything like that, though it does have an almost life-size elephant towering over one hole and a camper van blocking the route to another.

It also has skeletons in pirate costumes and holes that screech scornful comments when you miss a putt.

Regular golf is a daytime sport, but Jungle Rumble is open early in the morning until late, and it takes place in the dark, with neon painted objects throbbing around you, like a multicoloured migraine.

The overall impression is that you've accidentally stumbled into the head of a tripped-out John Lennon, circa 1967. Meanwhile loud music roars and bores into your brain – everything from Meat Loaf to Willie Nelson.

It's a slurry of surreal images, slippery surfaces and sloshing noise. And I'm at an immediate disadvantage, of course, as the cacophony of caterwauling crooners threatens to put me off my stroke.

"Lovely tunes they're playing," says the Nemesis, in a thinly veiled attempt at gamesmanship.

I ignore her and hit the ball.

At this point in the narrative, I should probably use my reporting skills to describe my putting stroke. But even Shakespeare, Milton and Peter Alliss, combined, would be hard-pressed to arrive at an apt metaphor to truly reflect the poetry, the majesty, the celestial glory of me whacking a small, dimpled ball.

But more important than my killer technique, after a couple of holes, I'm winning!

No, not just winning. I'm destroying my opponent, crushing her in the palm of my hand.

"Good shot, son!" says the Nemesis, attempting to lull me into a false sense of security.

Ha! As if.

I stride onwards, like Edmund Hillary making an assault

on the summit of Mount Everest. Okay, I'm only strolling up a gentle incline towards the next hole. But, hey, it's dark in here. I could give my ankle a nasty dunt if I don't watch out.

As the contest progresses, the Nemesis starts to eat into my once impressive lead. Though I'm not unduly concerned, because, unbeknown to her, I managed to do a little homework prior to the game. The previous day I "accidentally" interviewed the key people most intimately involved in the course we're playing.

Regrettably Kelly Meharry, the general manager of Jungle Rumble, proved as helpful as a seven-iron made out of freshly boiled spaghetti.

"I'm rubbish at mini-golf!" she admits. "My best score is up in the fifties."

Kelly plays every new member of staff to induct them into the ways of the course, and to a man and woman, they have beaten her.

Easily.

So, will she get the sack if she doesn't improve?

"I think everyone quite likes it, because I make the customers look good," she says.

Even Kelly's eight-year-old niece managed to annihilate her auntie. "The first time I let her win, because she'd never played before. But then she genuinely beat me."

And did Kelly have a tantrum?

"Too right! I won't play with her any more."

Meanwhile, back at the match, the Nemesis is now trailing me by only (gulp!) one point. Perhaps she's cheating. Not that I've seen her cheat. In fact, she looks entirely innocent. Which makes me even more certain she's cheating. After all, don't the most nefarious scallywags always appear innocent?

I'm still feeling fairly confident, however, because during my pre-match research I also managed to chat to Angus Wright, the 51-year-old owner of Jungle Rumble. Angus trained as a lawyer at the University of Glasgow, lives in St Andrews where he has a residents' ticket to play the Old Course, and also enjoys sailing.

Which makes him sound like a traditional sort of chap.

Yet he has been building defiantly daft mini-golf courses across the UK since launching the Jungle Rumble concept twelve years ago.

Does he also play the game? "When I was researching mini-golf, I visited a place called Myrtle Beach," he says. "It's a sort of mini-golf Mecca. I played two hundred holes in twenty-four hours, and haven't felt the urge to play much more since then."

Angus also designs the holes for his courses, though he doesn't rely entirely on his own imagination.

"There's a trade show for amusement park operators I attend every year," he explains. "Imagine a hall the size of Murrayfield, with all the latest rollercoasters, arcades and special effect ideas. It's a pretty mad couple of days.

"After the show I spend a few days going through everything I've seen, and then have to persuade my contractors that they can build what I want."

Angus has a good team behind him. When not working on his golf courses, they helped devise the fantasy sets for *Game of Thrones*, the TV show famous for outlandish and brutal deaths.

Talking of which, I've now managed to slay my own personal dragon.

Eighteen holes have been played, and the Nemesis is . . . defeated!

I've never been one to crow, or act in an unseemly manner. However, I do treat myself to a five-minute victory dance while whooping and hollering in the Nemesis's face.

"Well done, son!" she says, doing an excellent job of hiding her bitterness and fury, before adding: "Fancy a spot of lunch?"

"If you're paying," I reply.

Which she does, of course. Though I can't believe I had to ask.

With this constant level of antagonism, I'm regularly astounded that I grew up to be such a kind, generous and well-rounded individual.

16

A Dalek in its Death Throes

IN an earlier chapter of this book we revealed that the Scottish footy team didn't exactly dominate the Euros.

Though we did have a few decent matches outside of that competition. We even managed to draw 2–2 with Holland, which reminded the Diary of another historic occasion when our chaps battled against the Netherlands.

The 1978 World Cup finals in Argentina.

On that fabled occasion the diminutive figure of Archie Gemmill became a giant of a man, scoring a goal that has rightly taken its place in our nation's mythological mutterings, along with William Wallace's sword, Robert the Bruce's spider and Billy Connolly's big banana boots.

Archie skipped, slalomed and skedaddled past the opposition, leaving the dazzled Dutch to tilt at windmills. (Apologies for that last metaphor, faithful reader. But we're discussing Holland, after all, so felt duty-bound to include at least one clumsy windmill reference.)

The following chapter proves that we Scots do enjoy the occasional glimpse of Gemmill greatness.

Though invariably there's a pesky windmill waiting to block our path to glory . . .

WISDOM isn't necessarily conferred with a formal education, argues reader Norrie Patterson, who isn't enamoured by the process that guides an impressionable youth from the shadow of the nursery gate to the dreaming spires of university.

"Learning," he says, "is merely the process of going from playdough to Plato."

DURING a memorable Radio Scotland phone-in there is a heated discussion about school exams in the Covid era, with one caller saying: "Teachers have been working their socks off with one hand tied behind their backs."

The Diary can only guess what this cryptic phrase means.

Perhaps the material being used to bind teachers' hands is provided by those socks that are dropping off in such great numbers . . .

HOW about an updated English dictionary? A reader suggests: Hiberdating (verb): Someone who ignores all his/her friends when dating a girlfriend/boyfriend.

WE press on with our mission of improving the English dictionary with newly minted words.

A reader suggests: Errorist (noun): Someone who repeatedly makes dangerous mistakes.

THE Diary continues improving the English dictionary by adding words that don't already appear in it.

Jim Hamilton suggests: Unkeyboardinated (adj): Lacking physical or mental keyboard coordination; unable to type without repeatedly making mistakes.

DURING a weekend stroll, reader Darren Hogg passed an elderly gent riding a bicycle. The bike's owner must have attempted to change gears, for his contraption emitted a loud, pained, metallic screech, like a Dalek in its death throes.

"I've no idea why it's acting up now," muttered the fellow as he wobbled past. "I've only been riding it sixty-three years."

THE husband of reader Joanna Murray decided to assist her while she cooked dinner. His help mostly consisted of him glugging from a bottle of wine Joanna had bought to make a sauce.

"Well," said hubby, stoutly defending his culinary acumen, "the recipe says reduce the wine. And that's exactly what I'm doing."

A HERALD story about a *Watership Down* conference taking place at the University of Glasgow reminds us of the butcher who placed a sign in his window soon after the release of the movie, which is based on a novel about a gang of roving rabbits.

The sign read: "You've read the book. You've seen the film. Now come and eat the cast."

THE husband of Glasgow author Deedee Cuddihy decided to have a clothing cull. At one point he stumbled upon a pair of underpants he'd forgotten about, and that Deedee had never seen before. He explained that he bought them in a supermarket in France when the couple were holidaying years ago, but he only noticed the brand name afterwards. At which point he hid the undergarments, fearing Deedee would mock him mercilessly.

The pants were labelled: Dim.

And, yes. Deedee admits her hubby was most astute. She would have mocked him mercilessly.

THE slothful husband of reader Sue Cooper complained to her one day: "It's not fair. I go in the kitchen and I'm searching for food. But there's never any food. Just ingredients."

AN eagle-eyed reader spotted an intriguing registration plate on the M9 from Perth to Stirling, which was: OBI 1 KNB.

Our reader believes the car's owner must be a *Star Wars* fan from Glasgow, or thereabouts.

For it's only in the distinctive burr of the west of Scotland native that OBI 1 KNB becomes . . . Obi-Wan Kenobi.

COMEDIAN Andy Cameron gets in touch to tell us the following tale, which is very similar to a dramatic episode of TV medical show *Casualty*.

A wee Glesga punter is complaining to his doctor that he's got pains all over his body.

The doc says, "Show me where it's sore."

So the wee fella touches his shoulder and cries: "Ouch!"

He then touches his knee and cries: "Argh!"

Prodding his head, he yells "Oh, ya bass!"

The doctor says: "I see what's wrong."

"Is it serious?" asks the concerned patient.

"Not too bad," shrugs the doc. "You've broken your finger."

THE Herald Diary Book is perhaps the most sophisticated and urbane tome on the planet, which is why we insist that our readers peruse our series of *bons mots* while dressed in formal evening wear, a cocktail in one hand, a monocle covering an eye, and a cigarette holder balanced insouciantly on the lower lip.

Though sometimes we find ourselves straying into rougher terrain. For example, the subject of undergarments has cropped up, with a reader telling us the apocryphal tale of the starry-eyed young debutante who told her best friend after a night of passion with a new acquaintance: "I've been blessed. He had St Michael on his pants."

AN apocryphal tale involving a Hollywood legend and a chap named Wee Tam.

The setting for our story is a mythical town called Glasgow, a place very much like La La Land, only with double-decker buses outnumbering convertible sportscars and tartan bunnets more popular than Aviator sunglasses.

Our narrative commences when David Hasselhoff – famous for his TV role in *Baywatch* – swaggers into a local pub and orders a drink.

Why he's in Glasgow remains unclear. Filming a movie, perhaps. Or maybe enjoying the local weather and topping up his tan.

Delighted to welcome an acting icon into his pub, Wee Tam the barman says: "It's a pleasure tae serve ye, Mr Hasselhoff."

"Just call me Hoff," says the star.

"Sure," replies Tam. "Nae hassle . . . big man."

A DARWINIST diatribe from sweet-toothed reader Lucy Willis: "Chocolate is vital for our survival as a species. Dinosaurs didn't have chocolate and look what happened to them."

THE idiosyncrasies of the English language. A reader points out: "There's no egg in eggplant, no ham in hamburger and no apple or pine in pineapple."

WE continue exploring the paradoxes of our native tongue. Jim Dunlop from Largs notes that: "Quicksand can work slowly, boxing rings are square and a guinea pig is neither from Guinea nor is it a pig."

ANOTHER cockamamie contradiction in the lunatic lingo otherwise known as the English language. A reader points out that noses often run while feet may smell.

"CRYING over spilled milk isn't as common as crying because someone yelled at you for spilling the spilled milk," points out reader Lionel Bruce.

ON the subject of our era's most divisive political ideology, a reader points out that its roots can be traced back to modernist Irish literature.

"Didn't that Joyce guy write the definitive guide to political correctness?" he says. "You know ... *Finnegans Woke.*"

17

The Deep-Fried Pizza Awaits Your Pleasure

IT was famously once said by Marx (Karl, not Groucho) that history repeats itself. First as tragedy, then farce. The Diary doesn't agree with this proposition. Instead, we advance an alternative theory. History repeats itself. First as reality. Then reality TV.

In 2021 former Rangers star Paul Gascoigne became the latest high-profile figure to ramble down the well-remunerated reality route when he appeared on the Italian version of *I'm A Celebrity, Get Me Out of Here.*

Most people probably assume reality TV is a relatively new concept, though its roots can actually be traced all the way back to the Herald Diary.

Folk squabbling, folk committing unpardonable sins, folk confronted by public humiliation . . .

It's not just on your telly. Such shocking, sordid stuff can be found in the Herald Diary every day of the week. (Except Sundays, the Diary team's official day of rest, which we deem to be a shenanigan-free zone.)

As the following stories make clear, we never tire of reporting on humanity's inner weakness and outer wackiness . . .

A TALE of a flummoxed film fan. A chap took his girlfriend to the multiplex cinema in Hamilton, having imbibed a few jars beforehand. Flashing his credit card, he asked the lady at the desk for two tickets for *Man in a Trance*.

The lady helpfully informed him that the use of the *Main Entrance* was free of charge.

A WHILE ago singer-songwriter Bob Dylan won the Nobel Prize for Literature. The Diary believes that if a croak-voiced crooner can bag such a prestigious award it should also be handed over to the prolific author writing all those witty slogans on T-shirts.

A reader agrees, having been impressed by a woman on Stonehaven beach, whose T-shirt read: "I'm a vegan from my head tomatoes."

AN observant reader spots a St Andrews bike shop called Cyclepath, and wonders if it's popular with local under-graduates studying Psychleology.

"YOU know you're getting old," sighs reader Martha Brown, "when you actually start enjoying the lettuce and tomato on a hamburger."

BEARSDEN is one of Scotland's swankier suburbs, notes Malcolm Boyd from nearby Milngavie. A friend of his was working as a Bearsden catering manager. (A position known as a dinner lady in less salubrious areas.) This woman was stopped in the corridor one morning by a pupil who enquired what was on the menu.

"Sausages," she revealed.

"Oh goody!" replied the young scholar. He added that he was supposed to have had sausages for breakfast, but the au pair burned them.

A SCULPTURE titled *The Spirit of Kentigern* once stood in Glasgow's Buchanan Street. Reader Douglas Johnston recalls pausing to admire it when a young street urchin yelled, "Look mister, it's no' real," and proceeded to launch himself at the plinth, stone in hand, which he used to thump poor Kentigern. This resulted in an echoing boom, conclusively proving that the object was indeed hollow.

What ever happened to that persuasive street urchin, we are left to wonder.

One of the nation's most celebrated art critics, most likely.

A SPOOKY thought from reader Walter McCole: "A dyslexic ghost would really bamboozle any spiritualist trying to contact it using a Ouija Board."

ONE of reader Ben Glover's parents is from Cardiff. The other hails from Aberdeen. "Am I Scottish, or Scott-ish?" he wonders.

THOSE Australians are a wacky bunch. Some larrikin louts, desperate for a laugh in the city of Sydney, have painted on a rooftop near the local airport a message which reads: "Welcome to Perth."

Passengers glancing out the windows of descending planes are understandably horrified, believing they are landing in the wrong city.

The Diary wonders what message should be written on a rooftop near Glasgow Airport to provide a wicked welcome for landing passengers.

We suggest: "Welcome to Scotland. The deep-fried pizza awaits your pleasure . . ."

THINKING about the above story, David Donaldson tells us that if he lived near the flight path he'd simply paint a friendly greeting on his roof: "Hello there, China."

CANCEL culture has caught up with Enid Blyton, the children's author who wrote about Noddy and his Toytown chums from the 1940s until the early 60s.

Reader Guy Murray is delighted that Enid is ended. "It was unforgivable that the endeavours of Britain's noble and dynamic constabulary were disparaged by the introduction in Noddy of a character called PC Plod," he says.

"He should have been named 'PC Primed For Action'."

CHATTING with his wife, a reader happened to mention he'd been searching for some cheap flights on the Internet. She could hardly contain her delight and happily made hubby a celebratory cup of tea.

"I didn't even know she liked darts," says our reader.

WE are told of a medical sales rep who promoted a variety of surgical goods, including breast implants.

Upon being seated in a restaurant with a group of chums, this chap thought he recognised a lady at another table. A look of recognition also flashed across her face.

Just as he realised she was one of the operating theatre sisters he dealt with, she clicked at the same time, and announced in a loud voice: "You're the man who handles breasts."

IN the late 1960s and early 70s Tom Bain from Uddingston was working in Queen Street. The surrounding area was the centre of the burgeoning rag trade, and some young entrepreneurs were obviously making lots of money as there were a number of flash cars around. One had the number plate 1UPU, which was trumped a few weeks later by another motor with the registration UPU 2.

BEING an identical twin has advantages and disadvantages, admits a reader. "When I was giving the best man's speech at my twin brother's wedding," he recalls, "I said that I was not only saying farewell to my brother, but also to half my wardrobe."

Our reader's friend, who is also a twin, claimed he had that story beat.

Giving a speech at his twin brother's wedding, this chap admitted he was rather looking forward to the honeymoon . . .

(We believe in economic theory this sort of malarkey is referred to as the Division of Labour.)

THE youngest granddaughter of a reader has decided to enter a story competition.

The eight-year-old sent her grandpa the latest draft of the narrative she intends to submit, which features a French girl called Florence d'Etoile.

She meets Death, who tells her that he would prefer to be called Gary for the understandable reason that: "It's the best name ever."

A RATHER rum tale appeared in the populist press shining an unforgiving spotlight on a couple who were fined after being caught breaking lockdown rules while engaged in a tempestuous manoeuvre of the non-monastic variety. (In a motorcar, no less.)

This amorous activity was described in the newspaper, utilising the very highest of literary styles, as a bit of "rumpy-pumpy".

Which surprised one reader, who says: "I thought rumpy-pumpy was a term that had fallen out of use. Though maybe that's because I've reached the stage of life where it's all mumpy-grumpy."

THE worst type of neighbour to discover across the garden fence would probably be a drummer specialising in heavy metal music.

Though London-based Scottish broadcaster Zara Janjua has found herself living side-by-side with a non-drumming chap who also knows how to dish out the decibels.

An opera singer.

A rather trepidatious Zara requested that he cork the cacophony for an hour while she completed a recording she was working on for an event.

With a sigh of relief, she adds: "We spent an hour chatting and he gave me a bottle of wine. If Carlsberg did disputes . . ."

OUR readers are so dynamic, devil-may-care and driven by wanderlust that when they finish reading the Diary in *The Herald* of a morning they often proceed to constructing paper aeroplanes made from the page it appears in, which they then launch across the breakfast table.

Though sometimes our correspondents exaggerate their outlandish reminiscences . . . just a tad.

For example, a reader informs us that his grandad was bereft of financial liquidity and couldn't afford a glass eye, so visited the local carpenter who made him one out of teak.

Defending the essential veracity of his tale, our reader adds: "I wouldn't make a joke about that, wood eye?"

18

Grand Vizier of Vainglorious Verbiage

IN 2021 TV star Sam Heughan revealed he believes aliens have visited Earth. Sam has a lot of experience regarding weird happenings as he's the leading man in *Outlander*, a time-travel show set in Scotland. (Think *Doctor Who* with sporrans and tins of shortbread chucked into the mix.)

The Diary is sceptical when it comes to visitations from other planets. After all, if you were a Little Green Man with a flash flying saucer, would you really waste time visiting a sleepy backwater like Earth?

That's like owning a top of the range Maserati and only using it to drive the kids to school.

Besides, do we really need aliens in our lives? As the following chapter proves, life on Planet Scotia is strange enough, even without a visit from ET or the Cybermen.

A TRUE tale of hard times and social deprivation on the mean streets of Glasgow's West End, where one of the residents happens to be in possession of a large deep freeze which can store hefty hunks of meat. This resident also has a child who is playing outside at the very moment we join the scene, just in time to overhear the following exchange . . .

"Come in, Torquil. Dinner's ready."

"What are we having?"

"Venison."

"Oh no! Not deer AGAIN!"

A YOUNG policeman in Greenock wrote up a report regarding the disappearance of what he described as "home-ing" pigeons.

Having checked the paperwork, the youngster's sergeant called him over to explain there is no "e" in homing. The bobby replied, "Oh? Well there's no f in pigeons, either. They've been stolen."

OUR mention of stolen homing pigeons brings out the pedantic streak in reader Brian Chrystal. "Can you steal a homing pigeon?" he enquires. "Don't they just go back where they came from? Otherwise, they're just pigeons."

A TOOTHY tale. An elderly fellow from Giffnock had one of his few remaining teeth yanked by the dentist.

His young granddaughter tried to make him feel better about his tragic loss by explaining that at least he had a visit from the Tooth Fairy to look forward to.

"If the Tooth Fairy doled out dosh for every tooth I'm missing," grumbled Gramps, "he'd be in administration by now."

WE turn to the subject of distinctive fashion sensibilities as we recall the lady visitor to the Highlands who enquired of a chap: "Is anything worn under your kilt?"

To which the chap proudly responded: "No, missus. It's all in workin' order."

"CRUNCHY black toast would vanish as a staple of the traditional Scottish breakfast," predicts reader Scott Richardson, "if only someone would invent a toaster made out of glass."

GAZING admiringly at the wondrous vista that is his garden, reader Gordon McRae's eyes alighted upon a swathe of buttercups, which reminded him of his gran, who said you could tell if someone liked butter by holding a buttercup under their chin.

"It caused me to wonder if this applies to vegans," says Gordon, "or would they just claim a false positive?"

A FORMER colleague of a Hamilton reader was fond of the sound of his own voice. Being a generous chap, he also liked sharing his dulcet tones with anybody in earshot.

One day, after he'd delivered a particularly meandering monologue, a fellow worker interrupted this Grand Vizier of Vainglorious Verbiage.

"Sir," said he, "you are the type of person who runs out of useful things to say an hour before you stop talking."

WITH exam results arriving just in time to ruin teenagers' summer holidays, reader Ralph McBride asked his son how he thought he'd done in his subjects.

"Brilliant!" beamed the boastful boy, making his parent swell with pride.

Though Dad's delight dissolved rapidly when his son added: "I'm 110 per cent certain I got an A in maths."

VISITING his local pub, reader Glenn Lawes overheard a woman at the next table telling her gal pal that she adored the pop star, Beyoncé. Shrugging her shoulders, the gal pal said, "Whatever floats your boat."

"No," replied the first woman, "that's buoyancy."

BLOWING the dust off the keys on her laptop, reader Karen Logan has decided to write down all the things she ought to do, but seldom gets round to even starting.

"It's my oughtobiography," she explains.

MEDIA scholars will inform you that not all journalism involves drinking in the pub, thinking in the pub, and thinking about drinking in the pub.

Occasionally work gets done in newsrooms. (Once all other avenues have been explored, of course.)

Some heroic hacks spend lengthy parts of each day devising witty headlines to delight and dazzle their readership.

We were particularly impressed by a recent example of this artform which appeared in a *New York Times* article about Moray eels, who apparently can hunt on land.

The headline was . . .

"When an Eel Climbs a Ramp to Eat Squid From a Clamp, That's a Moray."

THE above entry reminds Gordon Fisher from Stewarton of a story that ran in the *Ulster Gazette* about a railway consultation exercise.

The headline was: "Over £100 million? Is This The Rail

Price? Is This Just Fantasy? Caught Up In Land Buys. No Escape From Bureaucracy."

WE continue celebrating memorable newspaper headlines. Ralph Baxter recalls one example of the craft he spotted roughly twenty years ago, which read:

"Statistics Show That Teen Pregnancy Drops Off Significantly After Age 25."

Not especially newsworthy, perhaps. Yet impossible not to admire such an astute scientific observation.

ANOTHER nifty newspaper headline. Reader Norman Lawson recalls one printed in the Second World War, which might have been the turning point in the conflict: "French Push Bottles up 2,000 Germans."

READER Norman Lawson recalls another classic from the Second World War, when a local paper seemed to boldly claim that one of the era's heroes had some trouser trouble.

The headline stated: "Monty Flies Back To Front."

ANOTHER tale of a newspaper headline with a muddled message. The father of Christopher Ide from East Renfrewshire was a compositor on a local English newspaper.

He recalled one headline that combined the legal and the leggy: "Magistrates to Act on Indecent Shows."

READER George Brown recalls the time a streaker flounced across the pitch of a London football team. The Aberdeen *Evening Express*'s headline simply, yet accurately, read: "Arsenal."

THERE are many stores in Scotland with names that are just as colourful as the goods they sell. Margaret Thomson tells us there is an Orkney dress shop on Kirkwall's Main Street called . . . Klaize.

THE husband of reader Mary Jamieson was typing on his computer in a coffee shop when he spotted a suspicious chap.

"He was sat on his own with no mobile phone or laptop to be seen," hubby later recalled, adding with a shudder: "Do you think he was one of those weirdos who go to a coffee shop to drink coffee?"

THE above tale reminds reader Julie Truster of being in a Starbucks queue in Glasgow city centre at 8.30 a.m., when an exhausted-looking chap in front of her ordered a milky coffee to take away.

The kindly barista studied the bags under his customer's eyes (which looked more like bulging suitcases) and asked if he wanted an extra shot in his coffee to perk him up.

"Not me," replied the customer. "I start work in twenty-five minutes, and the less my brain knows about it, the better."

FITNESS fan Jenny Minter says: "I wonder how many calories I'll burn while I'm running away from my problems?"

SHOPPING in Sainsbury's, reader Maureen Whitworth came across a staff member swishing a broom into the narrow gap between the base of a shelf and the floor. This action unearthed goodies that had probably been lurking there for ages. Musty tubes of Pringles, ancient Pot Noodles, cobweb-coated crisp packets.

An elderly chap toddling past while this was happening nodded to the shop assistant, and said: "Lord Lucan turned up yet?"

THE 50th anniversary of the opening of the Erskine Bridge reminds John McMenemy from Milngavie of the time an oil rig collided with the road deck in 1996. John happened to be travelling over the bridge a short while after the incident. Naturally he was filled with trepidation.

John's father, who was driving, attempted to alleviate his son's fears by reminding him that if anything did go wrong, there was an aunt in Old Kilpatrick (directly below the bridge), who was always saying: "Drop in any time."

FEELING rather sad that words like "milliner", "draper" and "hosier" are fading from common usage, David Donaldson was reminded of a story told by Glasgow artist and musician Al Fleming.

A number of years back, when Mellis the cheese shop was getting fitted out, a friend of Al's was sitting on a bus behind a couple of Glesga wifies.

The new shop attracted their attention, and one read out the shop name: "Mellis – Cheesemonger."

To which the other auld dear said: "A wunner whit they'll be sellin?"

OUR mention of a Glasgow cheese shop reminds reader Dave Johnson of the time he strolled past a similar store in the city's West End, late at night. Two tipsy student types, who had clearly staggered out of a nearby pub, glanced at the Cheesemonger sign over the door. One said to the other: "I've no idea how you monger a cheese. But it sounds painful, and I bet the cheese isn't a willing participant."

YET again we delve deep into the dizzying daffiness that is the English language. Jim Hamilton points out that the words "jail" and "prison" are synonyms. But "jailor" and "prisoner" are antonyms.

WELL-travelled reader Murray Gilmour has noticed that people who live in tropical climes tend to be a little more prone to nervous and excitable behaviour than those from chillier locales.

"Perhaps this is because so many people in hot countries have ceiling-fans in their houses," he muses. "And they realise, with fear and trepidation, that it only takes the shoddy workmanship of one ceiling-fan installer and they'll unexpectedly find themselves reliving the last moments on earth of Marie Antoinette."

VISITING a Barr's processing centre, the Queen declined a sip of the firm's legendary Irn-Bru beverage. "Her Majesty is meant to be politically neutral," points out Rob Young, "but this is a clear sign that she prefers the original Irn-Bru recipe to the new one."

Our reader adds: "If this isn't a constitutional crisis, what is?"

WE noted that the Queen refused a sip of Irn-Bru while visiting a Barr's plant in Scotland. A reader has a theory why Her Maj declined.

He believes our Head of State must have watched a TV interview involving Oprah Winfrey, a woman called Meghan and some grumpy English bloke.

Immediately afterwards she went off all things that could possibly be described as ginger.

AN outraged reader is determined to complain to a store about a wine box he purchased.

"The box says: 'once opened, will last eight weeks'," observes our reader. "But it only lasted three days."

A TALE of sleepiness and desire. Marion Carson from Dunblane tells us of a café in York that has a sign outside which reads: "A yawn is just a cry for coffee."

A PERTINENT and pugnacious point is made by sports fan Justin Simmons, who says: "If the heavyweight world championship is undisputed, then what's all the fighting about?"

ENERGETIC reader Hugh Dougherty was cycling through the plummier parts of Newton Mearns on a roasting hot day when he decided to stop for a rest. Strolling on the pavement opposite, an elderly couple nodded across to him.

"Saffy warm, as you'd never say up the Mearns," said Hugh, who lives down the road in the slightly humbler district of Cathcart.

"Actually," replied the man, with a straight face, "we'd simply say, up here, that the weather has a high calorific value."

VISITING his local chippy, Charles Black from Stirling was surprised at the high prices. Sharing his thoughts with the bloke behind the counter, he said: "Have you never heard of the phrase, 'Cheap as chips'?"

With a shrug of his shoulders, the serving chap replied: "That'll be them yins you cook in yer ain kitchen. When it's me dain' the cookin', ye hufftae pay extra. Cos I'm a fryin' pan genius."

IN the football chapter of this book we pointed out that Ally McCoist managed to slip the Scots word "outwith" into his Euros commentary, which was broadcast in all parts of the UK.

This magnificent victory for the Jock jargon reminds Eric Begbie from Stirling of the time the word furth – a Scots variant of the English term "forth" – sneaked its way into a 1950s Westminster Act of Parliament.

The Diary is now encouraging the Scots lingo to accelerate its invasion of the English language by stealth, never retreating until the Saltire banner is planted on the tip of every Anglo-Saxon tongue.

And we shall know our triumph is complete when Boris Johnson rises in the House of Commons, points to Kier Starmer, and says: "Oi, hingmy. Wit's the beef, pal?"

A LITERARY suggestion from reader Kevin Young, who says: "If you empty the pile of receipts in your wallet or purse and stack them together, it makes an itty-bitty book you can read, where the action-packed story is 'You versus Your Bank Account'."

"Spoiler Alert," adds Kevin. "This is one book that doesn't have a happy ending."

WHEN Patrick Murphy was in a coffee shop, he overheard an elderly lady say to her chum at the next table: "Well, I always say Sharon is exactly like my daughter, Ruth. Though, of course, Sharon doesn't look a bit like Ruth. And when it comes to personality, they're completely different, too."

NEWSPAPER hacks are a humble breed. Give them a byline, some booze and a bed for the night and they'll be content.

Usually.

Though occasionally a grander specimen stumbles into the trade, such as Hugo Rifkind, the regally named son of Edinburgh politician Sir Malcolm Rifkind.

The London-based scribbler and radio regular is feeling a little unheralded. "I know there's a lot of bad stuff going on in the world," he whimpers piteously. "But we're a family of four on day eight of a broken dishwasher with another six days until the repair man comes, and I honestly don't know why this isn't on the news."

WHEN exploring remote and exotic lands it's not unusual to stumble across a cryptic sign of grave portent. Les Reid from Edinburgh was driving alongside Strangford Lough in Northern Ireland when he spotted a huge boulder with "Prepare to meet thy maker" painted on it in big letters.

Fortunately, some helpful person had clarified the message by adding below: "Dress formal."

"Luckily I had a suit and tie with me," says Les.

19
Sassy Noodling

EARLIER this year I treated myself to a midlife crisis and bought a guitar.

She's a curvy little number and looks great resting on a stand in the corner of my living room, where she's become the ideal replacement for the exotic plant that previously stood in that spot until it died from a deficiency of sunlight, a dearth of water and overall heartlessness and neglect on my part.

But was I going to neglect Taylor Swift? (The name I've given my guitar.)

Hell, no.

Though never having learned to play a musical instrument of any kind, I wasn't yet in a position to woo Taylor.

So I decided to pounce on the world wide web instead, the place where you can learn anything about everything.

My Internet quest led me to a man delivering free guitar lessons on YouTube. He had a friendly smile, a laid-back manner and, most importantly, a guitar on his lap. The very bloke I was after. Or so it seemed. But when the lessons began I was as confused as a caveman attempting to complete a sudoku puzzle.

This guitar thingummy was a fiddle, a flummox and a faff-and-a-half. Much more complicated than it looks when Keith Richards is absentmindedly tweaking the strings of his Fender Telecaster.

So Taylor Swift and I decided to take a break from each other. Actually, I decided. Taylor wasn't so keen on my unilateral decision to have some time apart, and she started mocking me bitterly from her stand in the corner of the room.

"Ha!" said Taylor. "What kind of man are you anyway?"

"A man who knows his limitations," I replied, beer in hand. (Curiously enough, Taylor and I only ever had these conversations when I was enjoying a few alcoholic beverages.)

"A real man wouldn't give up on a relationship," she scolded. "He'd romance his guitar. Woo it, wow it, win it over."

I flashed Taylor my surliest sneer. "I never had this problem when it was a plant pot sitting in that corner," I hissed.

Unfortunately, Taylor's words wormed their way under my skin, which explains why, a few days later, you find me, faithful reader, on a visit to the First Chord Music School in Glasgow's West End.

Though not to strum a guitar. I'm still not ready for such a finger-flummoxing challenge. Instead, I opt for a ukulele lesson.

Now, you know when you watch a Cameron Diaz romcom, and Cameron's having bloke trouble, so she seeks advice from a quirky gal pal who is half Cameron's height, twice her weight and in possession of triple her share of chins? The gal pal whose sole purpose for existing is to stand next to Cameron, making Cameron look especially dazzling and unattainable?

Well, that's the relationship the uke has with the guitar – it's the sexier instrument's frumpy wee buddy.

Saying that, it's undeniably true that the uke has a few favourable qualities. It's cheaper to buy than a guitar, lighter to carry, and, most important of all, only has four strings (two less than a guitar!) meaning it should be easier to play.

At least that's what I'm hoping as I nervously enter the lair of the First Chord Music School, which lurks on Otago

Street. What's making me particularly nervous is that my limitations won't be hidden away in the relative obscurity of a private lesson.

There's an entire orchestra sharing the room with me. A group of musicians who regularly play gigs together. They perform as the First Chord Ukulele Orchestra, and their most recent showcase was in a Paisley church, where they apparently stormed it.

The musicians have varying levels of ability, though even those who are relatively new to the instrument seem to have a good idea of what they're doing. Some have been with the group for several years, and most have played a musical instrument of some distinction, if not the ukulele.

And me? I've never even accidentally coughed into the mouthpiece of a football referee's whistle.

I'm a musical virgin.

A migrant stowaway washed ashore on the faraway land of lilting tunes. Deprived of a passport or even the most rudimentary command of the native language.

In other words, I'm up a certain creek, and the only thing I have for a paddle is this daft-looking midget guitar.

Help.

I'd probably bolt for the door if it wasn't for everybody being so friendly, helpful and fun to be around.

They're a zany bunch, all right. Now I know that zany usually means loud, brash and under the misleading impression that you're a bit of a wag. But this lot are a genuine hoot.

Or maybe that should be hootenanny, because I'm informed that after today's lesson the gang are moseying down to Glasgow's country music venue, the Grand Ole Opry, for a boot scootin' bonding session.

To celebrate the occasion, one of the uke strummers, Alister McGhee, has arrived wearing a Stetson and sticky-on moustache, which makes him look like a dastardly hombre from a spaghetti western.

Alister's an intriguing character who hand-carved his own ukulele, which is an ornate and beautiful object with a little wooden creature crawling out its sound hole.

The uke I'm handed isn't nearly so fancy, but that's also true of my abilities, so I guess we're well suited.

The lesson takes place in December, so unsurprisingly, the tune we're learning is 'Last Christmas' by Wham!

Because I'm a newbie our tutor Finn Le Marinel gives me a few basic chords to strum, while the more proficient musicians get stuck into complex finger arrangements.

As simple as the chords are, I'm feeling pretty overawed. I usually only use my fingers for battering computer keys or a bit of cellphone fumbling. My digits are cumbersome and clumsy beasts, as easy to manipulate as Stonehenge menhirs.

I also don't like the fact I'm doing all my learning in public. My inner eejit is on full display. Thank goodness for Sophie Kromholz, who is also helping to teach the lesson. Sitting next to me, she continually boosts my confidence, helps with my finger positioning, and lightens the mood with wacky comments. "Give it some sassy noodling!" she orders.

I do my best.

Josh Foster, the uke strummer on my other side, helps too, by handing me a different ukulele to play. It's slightly larger than the one I initially used, making it easier for my faltering fingers to grapple with the strings.

Josh owns many ukes. He carries three on his person. "I've got Ukulele Acquisition Syndrome," he tells me. "Look it up. It's a real thing."

The evening ends with the orchestra giving a fine rendition of 'Last Christmas'. I do my bit. (A very bitty bit, I must admit.)

Then the friendly bunch of musos invites me to accompany them to the Grand Ole Opry.

Regretfully I decline, and not only because I don't have a natty Stetson hat and fake moustache to call my own.

The truth is that I want to get home as fast as humanly possible, to inform Taylor Swift that she's chucked for good.

From now on, I'm a ukulele man all the way.

20

Messi-ng Around

LIONEL Messi is arguably the greatest non-Scotsman to ever kick a football. Some controversialists even claim he is the greatest sportsman – from anywhere – to ever kick a football. Whichever theory is true, it's clear that the dinky Argentinian ain't too shabby.

Unlike the chaps who play for Brazilian side Íbis Sport Club, who may be the worst team in the world, having bagged a spot in the *Guinness World Records* for going nearly four years without a win.

That didn't prevent them from offering Messi a contract, on the condition that he admit Pelé is better than Maradona.

Messi hasn't responded yet, though the Diary advises him to do what's necessary, and sign immediately.

For as the following chapter goes some way to proving, life is more entertaining when you're hanging out with life's misfits, madcaps and muck-up merchants.

WHILE shopping, a Diary reader met an elderly neighbour in the supermarket, who was with her teenage granddaughter. Our reader mentioned that the girl looked just like her father.

"Don't worry, hen," said Grannie to the teen. "There's always make-up."

THE modern world is a nerve-racking place. Though reader Tom Law decided he needed more nightmares than usual to keep him tossing and turning in his bed. So he began researching viruses and stumbled upon a group of the nasty things called Pandoraviruses.

Thankfully, he tells us that they only appear to attack amoeba.

Even so, Tom hopes the Pandora strain stays safely locked in its – what's that thing called again? – ah, yes.

Its box.

LINGUISTICALLY lithe reader Bob Jamieson noticed that his partner tends to get her grammar garbled when it comes to singular and plural.

"When my wife says: 'We need to do something'," says Bob, "It invariably means that I have to do something."

A MENTION in *The Herald* of Jack Radcliffe reminds reader Ian Hutcheson of a story he heard the Lanarkshire comedian tell at the Alhambra theatre involving a drunk chap staggering home on a Friday night. A misstep on dismounting a pavement brought the boozer tumbling down heavily on his rear. Rising gingerly to his feet, he felt something trickling down the back of his leg from his hip. The sensation brought a prayer to his lips.

"I hope to God it's blood," he said.

A READER was chatting with a young assistant in a Byres Road shop. At one point in the conversation our reader said: "Well, you know what they say: A change is as good as a rest."

The shop assistant seemed puzzled. Our reader repeated herself.

"What?" said the befuddled clerk. "A change is as good as arrest?"

It transpired that, being a mere whippersnapper, the shop assistant had never heard the well-known expression from yesteryear.

Though he clearly knew what 'arrest' meant. Some words or phrases never seem to go out of fashion.

ANOTHER tale of shop assistants and their modern ways. James McGovern was in a supermarket with his wife. Not one of the better-known emporiums, we should add, where staff training is prioritised.

The couple were at the fruit and veg section when James's wife spotted a young assistant, resplendent in white workcoat and matching white trilby hat.

Said she to this spiffy chap: "Excuse me, do you have any celery?"

His response was immediate: "What the ****'s celery?" he enquired.

"Ten out of ten for candour," says our reader, approvingly.

IT'S time to go deep. Ocean deep. Thoughtful reader Kenny Carnell says: "How much deeper would the oceans of the world be if it wasn't for all the sponges floating about in them?"

COMMISERATIONS to Andy Murray, whose winning Wimbledon ways turned into wistful Wimbledon woes when his brave comeback in this year's competition crumbled into yet another setback.

Meanwhile, a reader believes that Andy's mum still has a glorious career ahead of her.

"Judy Murray should become Nicola Sturgeon's next policy czar," he argues. "With her wisdom and foresight she could be titled the Net Prophet."

THE daughter of a reader received an email from the local primary school which read:

"A time capsule was buried on the school grounds but no one seems to know where. It's the school's fiftieth year and they would love to open the time capsule to see what's in there. Does anyone remember it being buried? Any help gratefully received."

Alas, the Diary can offer no useful advice to the perplexed treasure hunters. Apart from something we were once told by a limping chap of our acquaintance, who went by the name of L. John Silver Esq.

This kindly fellow provided a three-point plan to obtain buried loot. His words are faithfully transcribed below . . .

1) Obtain a musty old map with a prominent X stamped upon it.
2) Purchase an ocean-ready galleon plus trusty crew. (Actually, they don't have to be particularly trusty. Though if they have advanced cutlass-waggling skills that's definitely a bonus.)
3) What are you waiting for? Get treasuring, me hearties.

AND so to Edinburgh, where a cleverly constructed marvel, the W Hotel, soars above the capital. Officially opening in 2022, it's topped by a prominent spiral.

The city's movers and shakers are desperately trying to persuade locals to fondly refer to this swirling edifice as the "Walnut Whip", referencing a popular chocolaty snack.

Regrettably a more scatological label is proving more popular, with one local scribe describing the building as: "Like nothing so much as what citizens are coyly enjoined to pick up after their dogs."

Reader David Black reports that there is now some debate regarding what initially inspired the architects. Some claim it was New York's Guggenheim. Others suggest Beijing's Bird's Nest Stadium.

"It's a difficult choice," says David. "Perhaps it falls between two stools."

METAPHYSICAL musings from reader Larry Jones, who says: "If reincarnation means coming back in a different body with no memories of who you were before, where exactly is the 're' bit of reincarnation?"

MORBID musings from reader Claire Owen who wonders what would be the worst way to begin a eulogy.

She suggests: "But first, a word from our sponsors . . ."

BOASTFUL reader Bob Hodgkinson tells us: "I'm great at multitasking. I can waste time, be unproductive, and procrastinate all at the same time."

EAGLE-eyed denizens of Glasgow may have noticed that the Dear Green Place is in the throes of an identity crises and has turned itself into the Dear Red, White and Blue Place.

America's national flag has been draped over numerous buildings in the town centre. But not to worry. It's all for a good cause.

Money.

And Hollywood money at that.

The latest Indiana Jones flick is filming scenes in Glasgow, which we presume is being used as a stand-in for an American city.

With its Glesga vibe, the Diary is curious to know what the completed movie will be called.

Bill Lindsay says that since the protagonist is played by 78-year-old Harrison Ford, who we're being asked to believe can perform all sorts of physically demanding heroics, it should be called: *Indiana Jones: Did Ye, Aye?*

ANOTHER suggestion . . . *Raiders of the Possilpark.*

OR perhaps . . . *Indiana Jones and the Templeton Carpet.*

A READER stumbles across the Indiana Jones gang filming in Renfield Street and realises he will probably giggle like a schoolboy if he glimpses the fedora-wearing, whip-cracking hero of his youth.

Though it seems that not everyone is a sucker for the escapades of an adventurous archaeologist. Our reader hears one elderly gent say to his wife: "Wit the hell's going on here, Jean?"

She explains the situation.

"Could they no' have done it somewhere else?" growls the exasperated gent. "This is a main road, for Chrissake!"

CONTINUING the movie theme . . . A reader notes that classic films like *Rocky* and *Star Wars* have had their ratings changed to soothe modern sensitivities. "Should Roy Rogers now come with a trigger warning?" he wonders.

WE hear that in East Kilbride parents are outraged that South Lanarkshire Council removed, without warning, a playpark situated in Hazelhead Park, citing the problem of vandalism as the reason.

The Diary is no expert on weighty council matters, though we do wonder if it might have been more beneficial to the local children to have removed the vandals while leaving the playpark intact.

THE Diary likes to boast that it is as deliciously daring as a flapper from the roaring twenties, giddy on bathtub gin.

Which explains why we occasionally publish tales about – brace yourself, gentle reader – nudity.

With this in mind, a correspondent asks: "Why do nudists smoke briar pipes?"

The answer is: "Because they've nae clays."

THE Rev Andrew Williams from Dundee tells us that some years ago one of his friends, a kirk elder, was working with young offenders. He took one of the young men to the General Assembly of the Church of Scotland.

The lad watched the proceedings as they progressed at a sedate and tranquil pace. He then asked: "Who's that in the big chair?"

The kirk elder explained it was the Moderator.

The young chap mulled over this information for a beat, then exclaimed: "Moderator? It's an accelerator you need."

21
Andy, Albert & Agamemnon

AFTER being delayed for a year, the Tokyo Olympics took place in 2021. Sport fans could finally enjoy ferociously competitive games of tig and elite level hide-and-seek. (At least that's what we assume took place. We didn't actually scrutinise the events in any great detail.)

Great sporting occasions are important for a nation's well-being. They remind us to never give up, always keep going, forging ahead till glory and gold are triumphantly seized.

And if that doesn't work there's always the option of stomping off home in a huff.

Meanwhile, there are no losers in the world of the Diary. Witness here our contributors as they (almost) always come up trumps, no matter the indignities heaped upon them.

SITCOM fan Gordon Wright enjoyed last year's *Two Doors Down* Christmas special and happened to say to his wife the next morning: "I've been lying in bed thinking about Doon Mackichan."

"About time," she replied. "The paint's in the lobby press."

ALWAYS on the lookout for a bargain, the Diary spotted a five-bedroom house for sale in leafy Coltbridge Terrace, Edinburgh, for over £900,000. Part of the deal was that the resident tortoise, who had lived in the gaff for over seventy years, would get to remain at the property.

We had only one question about this curious arrangement. Was the tortoise willing to pay half the mortgage?

For surely if it refused to shell out, then the shell should be forced out of the swanky pad.

TWO boozy blokes were spotted standing at a bar in Glasgow's East End. One of the blokes asked the barman for a glass of water. His chum looked at him disapprovingly.

The first bloke merely shrugged and said: "Sometimes I drink water to give my liver a nice wee surprise."

A READER decided to get an extension to his house. The chaps who worked on it were called Bob the builder, Eddie the electrician and Paul the plumber.

The Diary is now eager to discover if life always works out better when you only deal with professionals of an alliterative persuasion.

If this is indeed the case, we advise all our readers to only agree to visit the moon if the astronauts flying them there happen to be named Andy, Albert and Agamemnon.

RESPONDING to the above tale, a Largs reader says: "I would be happy to engage with Bet the Bookie and Thelma the Therapist, but would steer clear of Duff the Doctor."

A TELLY viewer stumbled upon a Channel 5 documentary about a train journey from Glasgow to Mallaig.

He was eager to watch it, especially as it was narrated by respected English actor Bill Nighy.

Alas, the viewer became irate when it transpired that the esteemed thespian couldn't pronounce "Lock" Lomond.

Nighy had even less luck with Tyndrum, Rannoch Moor and the Trossachs.

The telly viewer now hopes that babbling, bumbling Bill will be offered similar narration duties on a Welsh-themed programme.

He looks forward to Nighy's untutored tongue tripping over that wonderful Welsh word Llanfairpwllgwyngyllgogerychwyrndrobwllllantysiliogogogoch.

POSTSCRIPT: When we first published the above tale in *The Herald*, a reader got in touch to point out that we erroneously spelled Llanfairpwllgwyngyllgogerychwyrndrobwllllantysiliogogogoch as Llanfairpwllgwyngyllgogerchwyrndrobwllllantysiliogogogoch.

A foolish oversight. We really don't know how it slipped past us.

AMBLING round his garden with his three-year-old grandson, a reader pointed to some greenery and asked the little fellow if he could see the pretty flowers on the bush.

"Do you mean the bush in front of the agapanthus, Grandpa?" replied the lad, who is clearly shaping up nicely to become a mini Monty Don.

THE things people do for entertainment. Reader Pam Thompson arranged an amusing afternoon with some gal pals. The plan was to drop in at a wine bar, followed by a visit to a local psychic.

When the gang arrived at the fortune teller's house one of

the ladies, who was now rather tipsy, said to the mystic miss dealing the tarot cards: "So I'm guessing that I cross your palm with silver. You say something vague and meaningless. I conclude it's deep and profound. Then everyone toddles off home happy."

The psychic then proved herself to be an astute predicter of the future when she accurately prophesised that every single one of the gal pals would vacate the premises immediately, without having their fortunes told, which they duly did. (With the forceful encouragement of the psychic.)

AN observant reader spotted cookie cutters for sale that imprinted on biscuits a selection of tender messages capturing the warm-hearted spirit of our modern age.

Messages such as: "Stop talking", "I hope you choke" and "Please go die".

A DIARY tale about the confusing aspects of the English language reminds Brian Farish of demonstrations that were held in Edinburgh prior to the 1968 closure of the Corstorphine branch rail line.

At the time, the Edinburgh Transport Manager was named Ronald Cox and he stated that his buses could easily cope with the additional passengers displaced from the trains. The pro-rail demonstrators were outraged and within days the city was festooned with posters pugnaciously declaring: "Hands off Cox!"

TWO ladies were overheard chatting in a watering hole in Glasgow's West End by reader Cheryl Brennan.

"They say one glass a day is good for you," said the first lady, holding aloft her wine glass.

"True," replied her chum. "But they don't say how many times you should fill it up."

WE adore an inspirational tale involving positivity and personal improvement. Jennifer Brown from Paisley supplies us with one such narrative when she tells us: "Before my morning coffee I hate everyone."

Proving that obstacles truly can be overcome, she adds: "After my morning coffee I feel good about hating everyone."

ANOTHER story concerning those astute philosophers one often comes across in that academy of knowledge and wisdom also referred to as the local boozer. Reader Ken Hannan overheard one wobbly-legged chap at the bar mutter to another: "Y'know, people always say that everything happens for a reason."

The second fellow replied: "Aye, and sometimes the reason is yer a pure diddy who keeps screwin' up."

CONFUSED Martin Nevill gets in touch to say: "This guy at the furniture store told me that a sofa I was looking at would seat five people without any problems. The thing is," he muses. "I don't know five people without any problems."

22

Don't Play Down
the Qualities of Marmite

IT has been a disorientating year for our planet. For the first time in nearly seventy-one years the Earth was deprived of Richard Branson.

His beard was gone. His smug grin was gone. The bits of him attached to the beard and smug grin were gone.

The billionaire entrepreneur was fired into outer space on a rocket, only returning to earth after a truly epic journey.

Sorry, that's not quite right. He plunged back to earth an hour after leaving. So it was more of a jolly jaunt than an epic journey.

Perhaps he can be encouraged to blast into space again, staying a little longer this time. Maybe a decade or two.

The rest of us lesser mortals can keep our feet firmly planted on solid ground while helping Branson out by looking after his bank account and making sure all that lovely lolly doesn't get lonely.

Regrettably Branson never asks the Diary for advice. Though in the following chapter you'll see that we do deal with an awful lot of space cases . . .

STRATHAVEN resident Nan Livingstone reckoned she had come up with the perfect answer to a birthday present dilemma for a relative. She would order a bottle of single malt whisky from Amazon.

All seemed to be going as planned with the expensive cratur delivered on time. But there was a problem. The young fellow who brought the whisky to Nan's door wasn't for handing it over without proof of age.

Nan explained to the young fellow that, unfortunately, she had neither passport nor driving licence. As a result the birthday bottle was returned to the depot whence it came.

"Now, you can understand that Amazon have a legal responsibility to make sure their customers are of age," says Nan. "But they may have been a little over cautious."

Nan Livingstone is ninety-eight years old.

PRINCE Harry first moved to America to gain some valuable privacy. Since then he's appeared on TV with Oprah Winfrey, been interviewed by James Corden, featured as a podcast guest and launched a prominent website and brand.

His latest noble attempt to fend off unwanted attention is

to write a memoir. Reader Debbie Orton says:

"If Harry ever asks me to join him in a game of hide-and-seek I'll have to respectfully decline as it'll be the most rubbish game ever. Instead of hiding in the wardrobe, or under the bed, Harry will be leaping up and down in the middle of the living room, screeching: 'Yoo-hoo! Over here! Shy and retiring Prince trying desperately hard not to be found!'"

VISITING a village pub in Argyll some years ago, a reader was surprised to spot a condom machine in the gents. Such machines were rare back then, and the word "condom" had only recently been accepted into common parlance. Looking closer at the machine, our reader noticed a disappointed person had scrawled on it: "This chewing gum is rubbish."

THE debatable delights of Marmite tend to divide the nation. Rose Morehouse tells us: "I recently won a competition for ten years' supply of Marmite. It was one jar."

THE disparaging comment on the previous page rouses Joe Knox to valiantly come to the defence of the traduced condiment. "Don't play down the qualities of Marmite as a cure for baldness," says Joe. "Spread it over your head and from a distance it looks like hair."

A DISTURBING revelation from reader Pete Hartley who informs us that 1980s pop icon Gary Numan is thirteen days older than actor Gary Oldman. "Surely this goes against the laws of nature?" says our dismayed correspondent.

A DIARY tale about a modern youth being confused by a traditional aphorism leads a reader to point out that there must be numerous classic proverbs that youngsters find baffling or outdated.

He concludes that we should replace fusty phrases with fresh-n-frisky new versions. For starters, he suggests: "One man's Quorn is another man's poison."

WE continue replacing fusty old aphorisms with fresh-n-frisky new phrases, more suited to modern times. A reader suggests: "A Rolling Stone gathers no Mrs."

WE hear of a chap who took his wife sailing. Fearing an emergency situation, he encouraged his missus to learn basic seamanship, such as the rudiments of navigation and how to use the VHF radio.

His wife showed scant interest in learning these intricacies, so to ensure her active participation, hubby described a worst-case scenario.

"What would you say on the VHF radio if I collapsed with a heart attack," he said, "and the coastguard asked you for your position?"

She replied rather smugly: "Rich widow."

EVERY now and then the bleary-eyed Diary looks itself in the mirror, doesn't like what it sees, then decides never to visit the pub again.

At such moments one of our correspondents will inevitably get in touch and regale us with some bar-room badinage, reminding us why we became hostage to the hostelry in the first place.

Such a time has arrived, with reader Tam Gooch revealing that he overheard a tipsy tippler at a bar saying to his pal: "That's the great thing about a wee whisky. It makes ye ready for anything."

"Wit dae ye mean by anything?" enquired his pal.

"Well, for starters," replied the first fellow, "it makes ye ready for another wee whisky."

AS has oft been mentioned, the Diary has an obsession with daffy doggy names. Which prompts reader Alasdair Sinclair to recall that his father as a boy named his hound after a well-known painkiller of the time. When anyone asked what the pooch's name was he would always be entertained by the bamboozled reaction to his reply: "Askit."

AN East Dunbartonshire resident was scrolling through websites when he stumbled upon the *Good Housekeeping* site, where there was a competition to win what was curiously described as a: "Poo Pourri Bundle."

"What a **** prize," concluded our reader.

"I ALMOST dropped my phone on my plush, carpeted floor," says reader Geoff Morgan. "Luckily I have super-speedy reflexes so was able to slap it into the wall instead."

A PHOTO published in *The Herald* of a vessel with a risqué name reminds a reader of a boat he spotted just outside Tobermory. It was called *Wet Dream*.

OUR local climate is as unpredictable as a rodeo horse on roller skates. That doesn't stop reader Martin Brown providing us with what he claims is an accurate guide to both the Scottish seasons and the native population's reaction to them . . .

Autumn: Nae fair. Rain. Wish it wis summer.

Winter: Aw naw. Snaw. Wish it wis summer.

Spring: Rain. Again. Wish it wis summer.

Summer: Pure swelterin' oot there, by ra way. Wish it wid rain.

WE continue to express our concern for Prince Harry, that shy and retiring chap who repeatedly contacts media outlets to remind anyone who may have forgotten about him how much he wants to be forgotten about.

Reader Dawn Larner says that in some respects it's a pity Harry is married.

"If he was single he could be a contestant on reality show *Love Island*," says Dawn. "Then he could meet other young people, much like him, desperately attempting to avoid fame by wearing skimpy beachwear and winching each other senseless in front of a TV crew."

A MENTION in *The Herald* of a popular fumigant inspires a Bishopbriggs reader to tell us of the Orange Order stalwart who said to his wife: "You can buy plug-in air fresheners, but there will be no potpourri in our home."

THE public sector can often be pompous in its pronouncements, points out reader Gordon Casely who tells us he regularly receives emails from the government's Rail Accident Investigation Branch.

One missive described "overspeeding trains between Laurencekirk and Portlethen".

Gordon is curious to know if such a thing exists as underspeeding.

Or perhaps even perfectamountspeeding . . .

23

Thrills, Spills & Loose-Leaf Tea

IN constitutional matters the Diary team has traditionally been agnostic when it comes to the Royal Family. Though a scandalous event in 2021 transformed us into staunch republicans.

Camilla, Duchess of Cornrwall, launched a book club where she revealed that the kind of literature she enjoys reading doesn't include – shock! horror! – the very volume you now hold in your hands.

How could she be so uncultured as to ignore the Diary? Does this mean that all the members of the Royal Family are equally bereft of taste? Must we conclude that the blue-blood brood are a boorish bunch?

We now begin to understand why Oliver Cromwell got miffed with Charles the First and gave him a short back-and-sides from which he never recovered.

Though perhaps it's not too late to show Camilla the error of her ways. Which is why we now present a selection of Diary tales whose literary merits are beyond dispute.

So brace yourself for action . . . adventure . . . and very posh tea.

A DUMBARTON taxi driver picked up a passenger who recalled being a paperboy in the 1970s. This chap once offered a rival paperboy the opportunity to buy his round for £70. The competing media mogul declined, stating he would only pay £30.

The two entrepreneurs eventually agreed to settle the matter in a way that would make any capitalist society proud. They would have "a square go", with the winner paying the amount he had proposed.

AN East Dunbartonshire resident was flicking through a magazine in a dentist's waiting room when he spotted a competition promoting bottles of Ned Wine as a prize. He imagined this must be a sprightly little vintage, best served chilled on a street corner, accompanied by deep-fried pizza and the promise of random violence to round off the perfect evening.

How disappointed he was to discover that Ned Wine is a celebrated plonk from New Zealand, with no connection to Scotland's shell-suit sophisticates whatsoever.

SURFING a diabetes website, reader Maurice Brown was surprised when it asked him if he accepted cookies. "Was that a trick question?" he wondered.

LEITH is such a salubrious district of Edinburgh that the residents actually use words like salubrious.

Plumbers were once called to this swanky neck of the woods to deal with a blocked kitchen sink. Had the owners poured hot chip fat down the drain? Au contraire.

The man of the house, who adores his Lapsang Souchong, had been unable to obtain his usual supply in tea-bag form, so switched to the loose-leaf variety.

"And that's the problem," explained the plumber, who discovered he'd been dumping the used leaves down the sink.

Loose-leaf tea, it transpires, is one of the most common causes of sink blockage. And Lapsang Souchong has exceedingly large leaves.

Does the humble Tetley devotee struggle with this issue? We think not.

FRIENDS of reader Moyna Gardner once tried a vegetarian diet. They later informed her: "It's not that the bottom falls out of your world. It's the other way round."

THE ever-helpful Diary has devised some simple phrases to replace obtuse legal terminology. We suggest:
   Not Guilty = Go home and don't do it again.
   Verdict Not Proven = Lucky you. You can keep the swag.

EDINBURGH University and the organisers of the city's Book Festival started an online course called How to Read a Novel.
   The Diary always assumed this wasn't a difficult task. You merely open the book and start flipping pages. (Not forgetting to occasionally glance at those pages while you flip.)

"MY friend and I always laugh about how competitive we both are," says reader Cameron Burton. "But I laugh more."

A TRIP to the shops can sometimes seem like a well-thumbed chapter of *Lady Chatterley's Lover*. Reader Paul H. Costello's father visited the local Spar where the assistant, who had just finished bagging some floury Aulds rolls, declared she was nipping out the back to: "Get de-floured quickly."

THE son of Willie Ferguson from Irvine is no fan of towering works of literary genius, which is why he has been known to berate his poor father for enjoying his *Herald* newspaper of a morning.

On the other hand, Willie's son does love the famous prog rock group Supertramp. He could hardly believe it when Willie pointed out that the sleeve of their 1979 album, *Breakfast in America*, features a picture of one of his musical heroes reading Scotland's very own *Herald* during breakfast in a café in the States.

"There's fewer catty comments during breakfast in Irvine nowadays," chuckles Willie.

THE above Supertramp story has persuaded reader Roger Stephens that all record covers could be improved if only they featured the world's greatest newspaper.

"Nirvana album *Nevermind* sports an image of a baby paddling underwater, with a U.S. dollar bill on a fishhook, just out of reach," notes Roger, who adds: "Replacing that dollar bill with a copy of *The Herald* would make a far more profound statement. It would also promote literacy among aquatic babies."

ON a similar note, reader Mick Rankin points out that the sleeve of a 1966 John Mayall & the Bluesbreakers album sports a photograph of a youthful guitarist named Eric Clapton, who is portrayed studying a copy of *The Beano*.

Clapton's reputation never recovered from this immature incident, and he was never heard of again.

How different rock history might have been if this Eric chappie had been proudly perusing a splendiferous *Herald* newspaper . . .

BEING of high moral standing, the Diary would never be the source of idle gossip and rumour. Though we are happy to publish other people's idle gossip and rumour. For instance, Stevie Campbell from Hamilton hears that heavy rainfall has created a new loch in Scotland which the government are considering calling Loch Down.

(We imagine it must be a very dull loch. A home for bored fish who watch Netflix and take Zoom calls all day long.)

IN the 1970s a chap was employed by an Ayrshire coal mine, though he was rather partial to a long lie-in among various other lethargic practices.

One morning he was summoned to the pit manager's office, where the boss said: "It has come to our attention that your poor attendance over the last year has meant you're averaging a paltry three-day week. Can you explain the reason for this?"

He replied: "Aye, sure. Cos twa will no' keep me."

USEFUL advice from reader Andy Spurling, who informs us there are two unwritten rules in life:
  1)
  2)

HOME-based hobbies are the happening thing, with plant-growing particularly popular. In the past, this meant chucking some water in the general direction of a clay pot, then forgetting about it until those frisky shoots and leaves turned dry and crumbly, like an Egyptian mummy who has mislaid its tube of moisturising cream.

But with more people spending long hours at home there's plenty of time to encourage greenery to grow, either through abject pleading or snarled threats. Some folk even resort to playing their plants music.

According to a survey undertaken by website Pointless Plants, the music of Scotland's Lewis Capaldi is the most popular for coaxing boomtime blooming.

The Diary's yet to determine whether the survey interviewed plant owners or their chatty vegetation.

Though we're guessing the plants would have preferred the tunes of The Hothouse Flowers or The Bluebells.

ONE of our correspondents took her teenage daughter for an optical test. Every aspect of the youngster's sight, including her ability to see out of the corner of her eye, was examined. Which led the youth to boast afterwards: "The optician says my profiterole vision's fine."

THE above story reminds reader James West of the time he took his twelve-year-old son to have his eyes checked. The little fellow was apt to worry about anything in the nature of a medical examination, and spent the previous evening scouring the Internet for ocular problems he feared he might be suffering from. One of the conditions he stumbled upon was glaucoma.

Which led the youngster to whisper to his father, just before his optical test began: "What happens if I have guacamole?"

A BRIEF flurry of snow in Glasgow led the six-year-old son of Maureen Phillips from Giffnock to ask Mummy if it meant a rainbow would soon appear.

"No," Mum replied. "That only happens after it rains."

"Will we get a snowbow, then?" enquired the little chap.

READER George Moore admits that he and his wife need to take a long, hard look at themselves. He reached this conclusion after his wife pointed to a picture of a lemon and asked their three-year-old what it was.

"It's for gin," he replied.

A LITTLE girl grew up on the Isle of Lewis where her father was a hotelier. One morning her mother informed her that the cook's dog Teddy had died. Surprisingly, the little girl took the sad news in her stride.

When asked some hours later by her mother if she wasn't upset about the demise of the wee dog she had been so fond of, the little girl burst into tears.

"I thought you said Daddy had died," she sobbed.

THERE was a manic depressive the Diary once heard about, who also happened to be a serial arsonist. When this fiery fellow died rather suddenly his father gave a moving eulogy, where at one point he said: "Although my son never smiled, he still managed to light up every room he entered."

THE elderly grandfather of a reader admitted to only one regret in life. "Sadly, I never raised hell," he sighed. "I didn't even give hell a wee shoogle."

MORE humiliation inspired by the demon drink. Richard Gault attended a parents' evening many years ago at Rockfield Primary School in Oban.

It was there that our reader spotted in glorious technicolour a drawing of him and his wife, which was accompanied by the caption: "My dad drinks Guinness and Mum has the occasional gin."

"I then realised why we were getting so many smiles when we entered the school," shudders Richard.

WHENEVER Gordon Casely faced a major expenditure, especially on a luxury item such as (yet another) large book or (yet another) bike, his late father would grin ruefully and say: "You know, son, you could spend more on strong drink and wild women."

Regrettably our reader chose to ignore such wise paternal advice.

A CHAP playing a boardgame with his ten-year-old son allowed the little fellow to read out all the questions. At one point the eager youngster declared that the next question was about "a one capon".

The father was momentarily stumped before realising he was being asked about a legendary gangster from old Chicago town . . . Al Capone.

AFTER a long period in lockdown, teenagers are back in full-time education. Reader Darren Smith is delighted as his fourteen-year-old son desperately needs to brush up on his language skills. Trying to recall the word "pilot", he came up with: "That guy who drives planes."

SHOPPING in a supermarket, reader Frank Derby spotted a chap grabbing tubes of Pringles, which he would shake violently before returning to the shelf. When this chap saw Frank glaring angrily at him, he explained: "I'm checking before I buy, and this lot are all full of broken crisps."

"No doubt because people keep shaking them," pointed out Frank.

IN the 1980s one of our correspondents employed a worker who told him about a friend of his who ran a small sewing unit. When things got too much for this chap, he would simply skedaddle to Glasgow Airport for the rest of the day to sit and watch the aeroplanes.

"He was a bit of a bam," noted the chap's friend. "But if he'd been rich, he would've been eccentric."

THE above story about the class-based distinction between a bam and an eccentric inspires a Largs reader to expound further on the grammatic terminology to use when discussing eejits.

He argues that it should go like this: "*I'm* an individual, *you're* an eccentric, and *he's* off his bloody head."

THE weather was doing its white-stuff-falling-from-the-sky thing again, forcing the Diary to contemplate the nitty and very gritty subject of gritters.

We concluded that these ice-erasing trucks should be given scholarly names to celebrate the fine work they do in preventing people from skiting on their bahookies. (For the amateurs among our readership, that's a meteorological term meaning to remain firm of foot in adverse weather conditions.)

Our inspired contributors came up with the following monikers for gritter trucks . . .

Of Ice And Men.

Piers Ploughman.

The Grittique of Pure Reason.

E = M8 Cleared.

The Great Gritsby.

Fahrenheit 32.

Brrrrrrrave New World.

Minus Nineteen Eighty-Four.

Ice Cold in Auchenshuggle.

FESTIVE scraps from the Christmas table often last well past the 25th of December, points out Glasgow North West MP Carol Monaghan, who spotted a tinfoil turkey tray being used by kids as a sledge in January.

A concerned Diary was left to ponder what the children of vegetarians use to whizz down icy slopes.

Repurposed lettuce leaves, perhaps?

GENDER fluidity is a much-discussed topic, especially among the younger generation, as Pauline Brown from Shawlands discovered during winter when she strolled into the garden to admire the creation that her seven-year-old daughter, Susan, had made from the snow.

Our reader was surprised to discover that the little girl had nabbed one of mum's best bras and hooked it round the feminine figure she had sculpted. "Look, Mum," giggled Susan. "My snowman's sno' a man."

STRUGGLING to walk the short distance from her car to the local Sainsbury's in the middle of winter proved precarious for reader Emma Murphy. "The ice coating the car park was smooth, unfortunately my journey across it was not," sighs Emma, who skittered, skited, scrambled then landed with a very unTorvill-and-Dean-like thump on the ground. (Judges' Scores: 0, 0 and 0.)

She later explained on the phone to her young granddaughter what had happened.

"Women's shoes should be made from the same material as cow hooves," said her granddaughter. "Cows never fall on their bums."

Grannie didn't respond to this zoological deduction. "Though I almost pointed out that cows invariably have more legs than I do," says Emma. "Plus, you rarely spot them grazing in Sainsbury's car park on a freezing cold afternoon."

ANOTHER tale of winter woes. The husband of reader Mary Kearney had no inclination to brave the icy outdoors.

Instead, he entertained himself by standing at his living-room window, spying on pedestrians as they struggled to traverse the frozen path on the other side of his garden fence.

He particularly delighted in watching haughty joggers slip, slide then collapse in a heap of their own hubris.

Though he was less amused when people strolled on the grass verge next to the path, allowing greater purchase for unsteady feet.

On one such occasion he barked with outrage: "Come off it, that's cheating. You'll never fall on your a**e like that."

24
A Smidgen of Oprah Winfrey

TONY Blair was the Mr Optimism of British politics, gliding into Downing Street accompanied by the jaunty jingle 'Things Can Only Get Better'.

And things did indeed get better. For Tony's son Euan, at any rate. In 2021 his company was valued at £140 million.

Euan's own share of the loot was worth about £70 million – dollops of dosh that would give any chap's wallet a hernia.

We must admit that we were a tad envious when we heard about Euan's fortune. For we've been running a similar training organisation for years, with no comparable windfall. Diary stories are published specifically for educational purposes. To coach people how to fumble the ball, bungle the opportunity, mess up, miss out and melt down.

That's why we encourage you to closely study the following tales, so you, too, can be as triumphantly silly as our contributors.

CURIOUS reader John Delaney asks: "Do Spanish folk sit in front of the telly watching *A Place in the Wind and Rain?*"

COMEDIAN Andy Cameron was in a GP's waiting room some years ago. (The chap he was there to see was a Dr McMillan, whose son would later change his name to Robbie Coltrane. Sadly, we've no idea what became of this Coltrane fellow.)

In the waiting room Andy noticed a wee bloke picking up a copy of *The Lancet*, which led to the following conversation between the bloke and his beloved.

Wife: Whit dae you want wi *The Lancet?*

Bloke: Ah like tae try the competition.

Wife: Whit competition?

Bloke: Spot the boil.

THE fifteen-year-old daughter of reader Lynn Blackstone was looking depressed. Mum asked what was the matter. "I'm having a midlife crisis," replied the morose teen.

Mum pointed out that she was rather young for such an experience.

"I've no idea which part of my life will be the midpoint," responded the teen. "So I'm spreading the crises around a bit."

A WEE dram of bar-room badinage, courtesy of reader Robbie Duncan, who was in a Brodick watering hole one lunchtime to see Bobby the barman take two bowls of soup to a foreign couple.

"I ken youse don't speak good English," Bobby said to them, "but watch the soup. It's fair bielin."

AN inquisitive reader says: "I hate when a couple argue in public and I miss the beginning, then don't know whose side I'm on."

A HERALD article about mittens reminds reader Jean Waters of the time she chatted to an Aberdonian friend about woolly handwarmers.

Jean referred to mittens as poccies.

"Poccies?" said her friend. "What a funny name for mittens."

Jean enquired what her friend called them.

"Hummel doddies," came the reply.

HAVING never attempted a proper day's work in our lives, the Diary team has an insatiable curiosity about other people's careers. A reader recently spotted that the University of Aberdeen employs an Executive Director of Advancement.

An intriguingly vague title. After all, doesn't all paid work involve some kind of advancing?

Unless you happen to be a professional ballroom dancer, of course. In which case spinning in circles is the preferred option.

ONE of our ever-vigilant correspondents sent us a picture of a plumber's van in Ayr. The name of the firm, emblazoned across the van's door, was Calm A Khazi. A scholarly reader noted that the name is more appropriate than we first realised, for kamikaze translates into English as "Divine Wind".

Something trained toilet technicians know a great deal about . . . though perhaps not always the divine kind.

IN a thoughtful mood, a reader says: "When one door closes and another door opens, you're probably in prison."

MEDICAL terminology can be most mysterious, and not just for the layman. A doctor from distant parts was working as a locum in an Ayrshire village. Confused by the local lingo, this chap asked colleagues during a coffee break what a patient meant when she said she was: "Jist hingin'."

A colleague didn't entirely quell the visiting doctor's confusion by explaining that the patient must be: "A wee bit peely-wally".

WE continue investigating the mysteries of medical terminology. John Carmichael from Broughty Ferry says that in Dundee the seriousness of an illness can be altered by rearranging the order of words. A person who is "No' affy weel" may simply have a bad cold, whereas if they are "Affy no' weel" the relatives are likely to be gathering at the bedside.

TOLSTOY famously wrote: "All happy families are alike. Each unhappy family is unhappy in its own way." The Royal Family's way of being unhappy is certainly distinctive, involving thrones, crowns, a stroppy red-haired fellow and a smidgen of Oprah Winfrey.

Even rock star Noel Gallagher has entered the fray, commiserating with Prince William for having such a woke snowflake for a brother.

Meanwhile, the Diary has decided to valiantly gallop to Harry's defence by pointing out that he's not the first blue-blood to exhibit a certain, erm, "uniqueness" in his thinking.

A reader recalls a tale which we certainly hope is true. It involves a certain Sandhurst instructor (and one-time husband of Princess Anne) named Mark Phillips, who apparently told his class of aspiring officers: "Humility is a virtue. It is important to be humile."

A CUSTOMER in a popular Wishaw watering hole handed his pint back to the barman, complaining that the beer was cloudy. Lifting the pint to the light, the barman explained that the beer was fine, it was the glass that was dirty. He then returned the drink to the customer, who happily gulped it down.

A READER gets in touch to tell us that he is regrettably not as sprightly as he once was. "I run like the winded," he sighs.

DESPITE this year's difficulties, bookshops recorded their highest sales for almost a decade. Reader Michael Harris says: "Customers must have bought in bulk so they wouldn't only have flock wallpaper to sit in front of during Zoom calls."

THE Diary was sad to hear Edinburgh's landmark Princes Street store Jenners is to close after 183 years of trading.

Reader David Black reminisces about the days when you could tell an Edinburgh lady by the cut of her fur coat, and a gent by the size of his Dundreary whiskers. An era when Jenners emporium was the *crème de la crème* of upmarket department stores, where only the elite could afford to shop. Those with aspirations, though lacking the necessary means, often visited the much less exclusive J&R Allan on South Bridge Street.

Thus, when faced with the question: "Och, where did you get that lovely het, Senga?" one might salvage some social credit with the slurred reply: "Oh, it was Jay an Rs, Betty."

OUR tale about Jenners closing reminds a reader that it was a complicated shop to navigate. One of his old acquaintances never got over the shock of losing his kids during a visit, many years ago.

He recently said: "Maybe they'll find them during the clear out."

OUR discussion about Edinburgh's grand old emporium, Jenners, reminds reader Gordon Kerr of his late Edinburgh auntie, who called the store "Morningside North" and insisted the tea room didn't have the aroma of freshly baked scones, but overwhelmingly of White Linen perfume.

Shall we see the splendiferous likes of Jenners on the high street again? the Diary wonders. Alas, not likely . . . unless Poundland commits to a daringly radical change in its current marketing strategy.

PUZZLED Rab Henderson from Falkirk wants to know if members of The Flat Earth Society ever go on Round the World cruises.

A PAL of reader Fred Robertson still enjoys whizzing around on a skateboard, even though he's forty-seven years old.

Fred enquired if it wasn't time he hung up his wheels and found a more mature mode of transport. "Good idea," said the pal. "I've always wanted to try a Space Hopper."

WE published a picture of an incorrectly spelled sign, which leads reader Brendan Keenan to rush to the defence of whoever wrote the message.

Brendan used to work for Dumbreck Decorators, where the policy was to teach apprentices to write "WAT PAINT" or "WET PIANT" on outdoor jobs.

The reason being that passers-by would notice the mistake and be more likely to heed the message.

Wonky spelling – it reelly kapchurz thi atenshun.

THE above tale inspired David Miller from Milngavie to get in touch. "It deosn't mttaer in waht oredr the ltteers in a wrod are wirtten, so lnog as the fisrt and lsat ltteers are in the rghit pclae," he explains.

As we understood every word of David's message, we suspect he might be rihgt.

WHEN Valentine's Day came around one of our romantic readers informed us that he had been thinking about those special people who mean so much.

"Sometimes, someone unexpected comes into your life out of nowhere, makes your heart race, and changes you forever," he sighed. "We call these people cops."

25
It'll Never Catch on in Kirrie

THE Diary thinks of itself as very much in the mould of the late John Lennon and Yoko Ono. And not only because we fervently believe that languishing in bed is a constructive way to spend the day. (Or week. Or month . . .)

Like John and Yoko, we want to give peace a chance. Which explains why we were shocked and saddened to hear of the binman sacked by Herefordshire council last winter after CCTV captured him on his round kung fu kicking a snowman. As far as we can ascertain, the snowman did not provoke the attack. Throughout the ordeal he remained icy-cool, calm and collected, never once losing his head. Until it was booted from his shoulders by the binman.

The following thoughtful stories prove that you don't have to get your kicks like a rough-n-tough refuse collector.

Instead, you can be supersmart.

Like spinach . . .

MANY years ago Ian Noble from Carstairs Village worked with a sales manager called Sidney, who was partial to a half-bottle of the hard stuff.

Sadly, he was admitted to hospital following a heart attack. A couple of weeks later Ian and a few colleagues were in the local enjoying their usual bar lunch – two pints and a packet of crisps – when in sauntered Sidney. He proceeded to order a large whisky, which he rapidly downed. It was immediately followed by another. And another. After he'd dispensed with his fourth, a concerned Ian suggested to the thirsty sales manager that he might be over-imbibing a tad.

With a flourish Sidney pulled his hospital discharge letter from his pocket and pointed to the advice contained therein, which stated: "A small refreshment is permitted."

THE world is run by computers containing vast amounts of our personal information. To protect this top-secret info from prying eyes we are often asked to devise password security questions. Reader Calum Sedgman, who is experiencing a certain amount of ennui at the moment, has devised some nihilistic password security questions to suit his mood . . .
   1) On what dank alleyway did you first lose your child-hood sense of wonder?
   2) When did you first stop trying?

FRUSTRATED reader Marc Oliver says: "Autocorrect has become my worst enema."

ENGLISH ballet dancer Darcey Bussell is proud of her Scottish roots. "My grandfather used to take me to ceilidhs, and learning Scottish and Irish dancing was an important part of my education as a professional dancer," she recalls.

Perhaps Darcey could combine her love of Celtic jigging with the style that made her famous. The Diary would happily purchase front-row tickets to watch her version of *Swan Loch*. Or instead of *The Nutcracker*, Dame Darcey could cut a dash in *The Heedbanger*.

DISGRUNTLED security guard Ted Bruce wasn't pleased when his boss asked him to watch the office.

"To be honest, I've never been a huge fan of Ricky Gervais," he told his boss.

THE sighting of a humpback whale in the Firth of Forth delights reader Lucy Davies, though she is less happy about the label that we nasty humans impose on such proud beasts of the sea.

"Wouldn't it be much kinder if instead of calling them humpback whales we called them whales with poor posture?" suggests Lucy.

ON a related topic, should we believe reader Sandy Tuckerman, who tells us he adores exotic dining and once visited an Inuit restaurant. On the menu were whale steaks, whale burgers, whale curry, whale stir fry and Vera Lynn.

Curiosity tweaked, Sandy asked the waiter what ingredients were in the Vera Lynn dish.

"Whale meat again," he replied.

THE above tale reminds Jim Allan from Cellardyke of his student days, when he was a resident of Glasgow Uni's MacBrayne Hall in Park Circus Place, and frequently joined in choruses of "whale meat again" when yet another meal was served by Matron, who stretched the meat allocation by using unrationed whale steak.

Our correspondent rather enjoyed the unusual flavour of the stews and grills conjured up with the meat, though he was definitely in the minority.

This was evidenced when an entry appeared in the Suggestions Book proposing that: "In future Matron should order the whales singly and not by the dozen."

TO Florida's SeaWorld, where a group of twelve-year-olds from Glasgow are paddling with dolphins while their chums watch. Each member of the party is allowed to get close to a dolphin to give it a wee kiss and a cuddle.

As one of the Glasgow kids prepares to do so, a friend sitting on a rock nearby shouts: "Hi Lizzie!"

Lizzie turns from the dolphin to her pal, who says sternly: "Nae tongues."

IT has been revealed that American scientists have taught spinach how to send emails. An important breakthrough, obviously, as it's not as though boffins have any greater concerns to engage them.

Though reader Marvin Clarke isn't impressed. "Teaching spinach to send emails is no big deal," he snorts. "It's not exactly rocket science, is it?"

ON the same subject, an unimpressed reader tells us there's nothing new about plant communication. "We've had SAGE telling us what to do for a year now," he points out.

CONTINUING with the topic of intelligent plant life, a reader gets in touch to say: "I'm now eagerly waiting for that first notification: 'You've got kale.'"

NOT all of our readers are impressed by our tale of super smart spinach. Alan Potter from Paisley shrugs his shoulders and says: "For years Sunday School children have known of the intellectual qualities of the plant world when they sang 'Lettuce With a Gladsome Mind'."

"GOLF is weird," claims reader Maurice Brown. "Vast areas of greenery dotted with little holes just because blokes are embarrassed to ask each other if they want to go for a stroll."

CURIOUS reader Laura Byrne asks: "Why is a group of squids not called a squad?"

A BLOKE is quizzing his young son. "What's the capital of the Ukraine?" he asks.

The youngster responds with a blank stare, so Dad gives him a clue.

"It gave its name to a chicken dish," he hints.

"Is it Tikka Masala?" enquires the boy.

OUR contributors often come from such poverty-stricken backgrounds that it would only need a sprinkling of flat caps, plus a jaunty song or two, to turn their humble childhoods into a Lionel Bart musical.

With a tear trickling down his cheek, Russell Smith from Largs recalls his own hardscrabble origins: "At school in the 1940s I had a friend whose family were so poor that he had a brother made in Hong Kong."

A TALE of agony and economy. The youngest son of Stevie Campbell from Hamilton is suffering from a repetitive strain injury in his hand.

Stevie showed much paternal concern by diagnosing the cause of this ailment as being a result of the lad's habit of dipping a paw in Pop's wallet.

The lad was unsatisfied with this prognosis and requested a second opinion.

Alas, the doctor agreed with dad and said the young man should have no more "hand doubts" in future.

A LINLITHGOW factory worker had a work colleague who often mentioned her friend Peggy, who wore numerous rings on her fingers.

One day the factory worker spotted her colleague in a café, chatting to a lady adorned with many rings.

"You must be Peggy," she said. "I've heard so much about you."

It was indeed the oft-mentioned Peggy, though she took umbrage at being referred to in such a manner and stormed out of the café.

It transpired that Peggy was not her given name, though the poor woman was in possession of a prosthetic leg. (And some very childish, nasty friends.)

IN the 1970s Robert Groves worked in McCormack's music shop in Glasgow. One day a young fellow and his mother

came in. The lad wanted a guitar and had very specific require-
ments regarding Fender Strat' or Gibson. His mum, not so
musically minded, ambled round the shop saying: "What
about that nice yellow one? Oooh, there's a lovely red one!"

The scarlet-faced young rocker turned to Robert and
hissed under his breath: "See maws? Maws should be shot."

THE above story reminds Mike Lennon of being eleven
years old and telling his father: "When I grow up I want to
be a rock star."

"Make up your mind," replied Dad. "You can't do both."

THINKING about the confusing words of hymns reminds
Nita Marr from East Lothian of Sunday school, where she
sang: "Till hosannas reach the skies."

"I thought hosannas were some kind of tree," admits Nita.

The Diary, being most wise and erudite, knows this is not
the case. A hosanna is a stepladder.

AIRDRIE Sheriff Court heard an impassioned plea from
a chap in the dock who wanted the court to show leniency
towards him as he had recently been offered a job as a post
cleaner.

The sheriff was a learned fellow, though he admitted that
he had never heard of this particular vocation.

On being told this, the chap in the dock went into whispered consultation with his lawyer. The lawyer then explained

to the sheriff that his client had assumed "post cleaner" to be the name of the work he would be undertaking.

What had actually been written down in the Job Centre advert was . . . Post: cleaner.

A FEW years ago, Gordon Fisher from Stewarton arranged to meet a pal for beers in Glasgow city centre, with both blokes intent on visiting a watering hole neither had been to before.

Gordon's friend mentioned he had spotted a new Italian wine bar which looked promising. "It's called Albarone's," he added.

The two chaps duly met at Central Station, then Gordon's chum guided him round the corner to be confronted by Scotland's premier Italian drinking establishment . . . All Bar One.

THE young daughter of Lee Beattie, the CEO of Glasgow-based public relations firm John Doe, was depressed when Valentine's Day was over for another year.

Lee tried to comfort the girl by saying: "But, darling, we all just love each other every day."

The youngster wasn't to be taken in by this slick PR campaign promoting the love brand and replied: "Oh, Mummy, it's not about loving each other. It's about presents."

SPOTTING a photograph in *The Herald* of men signing up as fire-watchers, a reader recalls the famous remark said to have been made by a new recruit: "Suppose there is a fire, how long should I watch it?"

FIFTY years ago decimalisation was foisted upon a confused and panicked nation, with shoppers and store owners grumbling to each other: "One hundred pence to the pound? Thar be witchcraft, so it be."

The husband of reader Ethel Fitzgerald from Perthshire tells the tale of being a young go-ahead director in his father's butcher business in Dundee when he was despatched to Kirriemuir to instruct the local butchers in the mysterious ways of the new money.

After the induction, one of the elderly butchers harrumphed: "Aw naw, son. It'll never catch on in Kirrie."

OUR readers continue recalling the advent of decimalisation, which shook our shilling-loving nation to the core.

Mary Duncan from Garrowhill recalls putting ten gallons of petrol in her car at the Eglinton Toll filling station in 1971, when the price was 33p a gallon. There were no automatic tills back then, so the girl at the counter was forced to write down '33' ten times in a column, which she proceeded to add up, eventually arriving at the total charge of £3.30.

ANOTHER tale of civilisational choas and decimalisation.

Comedian Andy Cameron tells us that his granny, Bella, got her provisions from Boabby's Biscuit Bus.

One day Boabby visited Bella's street and she came on the bus for a few bits and pieces.

"Boabby," said Bella, who was in her eighties at the time. "Gie's a quarter o' tomatoes, a hauf pun o' cheese and a hauf pun o' butter."

Boabby informed her that because the UK was now in the decimal age it was all kilos. "Well, gies a quarter pun o' kilos anaw," said Bella.

A POETIC reader recalls a rhyme he and his chums used to recite at school. (WARNING: We advise our refined and sophisticated readership not to peruse the following at the breakfast table.)

"Down the lavvy
Six foot deep
Lies a tollie
Fast asleep.
Do not touch it
Let it rest
Beecham's Pills
Have done their best."

OUR readers recall more scandalous verses devised during their misspent youth, with one contributor sharing a racy adaptation of the old Pepsodent toothpaste jingle:

"You'll wonder where your knickers went,
When your elastic bursts by accident."

[273]

ANOTHER variation on the old Pepsodent jingle . . .

"You'll wonder where your teeth have gone,

When you brush your teeth with an atom bomb."

(The youth of old must have been an optimistic bunch, for the Diary's contacts within the scientific community inform us that it's almost impossible to balance an atom bomb upon the bristles of your average toothbrush.)

ALONG with his school chums, a Largs reader would trill with religious fervour the following spiritual number, which celebrated his primary school headmaster:

"Old Bill he is a holy man,

He goes to the kirk on Sunday,

And prays to God to give him strength,

To belt the weans on Monday."

FORMER Labour MP, Sir Brian Donohoe, provides us with this daffy ditty:

"*Three wee girls at Leicester Square,*
Selling knickers at threepence a pair,
They're fantastic,
No elastic,
Not even fit to wear."

Having studied this verse closely, the Diary has now charged its crack team of reporters with investigating a glaring contradiction within the narrative.

If the knickers are indeed fantastic (even though they are *sans* elastic) how can they also be unfit to wear?

PET owner Charles Murphy was recently studying his dog.

"Look how easily amused that daft mutt is chasing its own tail," he chuckled to his wife.

"The dog's easily amused?" countered the missus. "He's not the one sat there watching a dog chase its tail."

26
Nut, Nut, Nut, Nut, Nut

WE did it! At long last the human race managed to escape the spinning ball of dust and misery that is planet Earth by landing on another spinning ball of dust and misery. Though for a refreshing change this one happened to be called Mars.

Full disclosure. When the Diary claims the "human race" fled to Mars, we don't actually mean that any member of Team Homo Sapiens made the journey during 2021. It was merely an unmanned hunk of metal that NASA casually lobbed into orbit, much as a boozy chap tosses an empty bag of pork scratchings into the gutter while staggering home from the pub.

The six-wheeled vehicle named Perseverance trundled round the barren soil of Mars searching for life, while undermining any hope of finding it by thoroughly polluting the atmosphere.

The Diary wonders why NASA bothers. Why search for new lifeforms when there are so many exotic specimens of humanity still to study on earth?

Evidence of which is amply provided forthwith . . .

THE renowned wit Samuel Johnson once claimed that patriotism is the last refuge of the scoundrel, which may be true when it comes to a person's relationship with the nation state.

But patriotism towards a city? Surely that is a fine and noble thing, says Glasgow-based writer Deedee Cuddihy, who is threatening to delete her eBay account owing to a message it sent to her explaining that her "approximate location" was Edinburgh, United Kingdom.

"I'm in Glasgow, eBay," growls Deedee. "Have you never heard of it?"

A CELLARDYKE reader has spotted a similar problem to the one above. Apple Maps have labelled a street in his hometown as East Fourth Street. Which sounds very hip and New Yorkish, though the street in question happens to run alongside the Firth of Forth . . .

"NASA landed a rover on Mars to search for signs of life," notes reader Andy Miller. "Hopefully they'll land a similar vehicle in the desolate landscape between Boris Johnson's ears."

THINKING about the joys of camping reminds a reader of the apocryphal tale about tent-makers Black's of Greenock.

It was claimed that one of their January sales was run under the slogan: "Now is the winter of our discount tents."

LADIES who phoned the Breastfeeding Unit at a certain Scottish hospital would sometimes be put on hold. They were then treated to the tune 'These Are My Mountains' while they waited to be connected.

THE English dictionary is an excellent book, though we wouldn't advise reading it cover-to-cover in one sitting. (If you're looking for edge-of-your-seat entertainment, best stick with the magnificent tome you currently hold in your hands.)

Even though the dictionary is a profound work of scholarship, we've noticed that many essential words don't appear in it. Which is why we occasionally feel it is our solemn duty, as one of the gatekeepers of knowledge in the UK, to demand new words be included.

With this in mind, a reader suggests "Sarchasm" (noun): The gulf between the author of sarcastic wit and the person who doesn't get it.

A GROUP of students planning to shoot a short film in Ayrshire advertised for actors to audition for the role of

Death. And what qualifications are required to play such an austere role? you may wonder.

Well, the film-making troupe said they were searching for a female, in her twenties or over, who has a driving licence, if possible.

The Diary was intrigued to discover that death is a damsel, not a dude. We also weren't aware that she drives to appointments. We're now curious to know what happens when the deathmobile breaks down.

Does the Grim Reaperess flag a cab, or does she prefer to patiently wait at the bus stop for the next double-decker of doom?

WE continue providing new definitions for old words. David Walker suggests: "Multivarious [noun]": A selection of routes from Tobermory.

FOR its residents, Glasgow is a fabled metropolis. As poetic as Paris, as dynamic as New York, as infused with mystery as Venice.

Regrettably, those who aren't natives of the city don't always think of it in such romantic terms. Sometimes they don't think of it at all. We've pointed out that according to eBay there is no Glasgow, just somewhere near Edinburgh.

Which reminds Mary Duncan from Garrowhill of a telephone conversation she had with a chap south of the border, who asked: "Is Glasgow in Scotland?"

Disgraceful. Though at least the fellow had actually heard of Glasgow.

And Scotland.

The education system in England is clearly on an upward trajectory . . .

THE grandmother of reader John Campbell once asked: "Who was that old English queen? You know, the one who ruled in the Victorian era."

DURING his time in the merchant navy a Milngavie reader sailed with a third mate known as Jumbo. At first our reader was confused by this madcap moniker as the chap, whose name was Les, wasn't overweight. The mystery was solved when our reader spotted Jumbo's signature.

It was L. E. Fant.

THE same reader once sailed with an engineer referred to as Harpic because everyone thought he was clean round the bend.

THE above two stories inspired our readers to bombard us with recollections of nifty nicknames. Here's just a few of them . . .

THERE was a senior official in North Lanarkshire who signed his correspondence "R. Slater". He was often referred to as "Heid First".

A KIRKCALDY reader worked with a chap called Milne, who turned the most simplistic job into a mammoth task.

"We called him Cecil B. on the grounds that he could make an epic out of anything," recalls our reader.

MANY years ago there was a science teacher at Bearsden Academy named Mr Henderson who was a religious man with hands like shovels. Inevitably, his pupils called him "Hands Christian Henderson".

AT school Bob Byiers had a science teacher called William Williams. The mathematically minded schoolchildren in his charge dubbed the poor chap "Bill Squared".

FORMER Gourock High School pupils may recall an older member of staff known for disappearing into a walk-in cupboard in his classroom, whence would billow a puff of smoke, accompanied by a strong smell of pipe tobacco.

This chap was charged with the task of imparting knowledge of both geography and English, which earned him the nickname "Vasco da Grammar".

WHEN John Mulholland was a schoolboy he participated in a religious education lesson which focused on the dilemma faced by Pontius Pilate, who asked the crowd to decide which prisoner to free at the Passover Feast.

"If you were in the crowd that day, who would you have set free?" asked the teacher.

"Jesus!" shouted twenty-nine voices in unison.

Though one boy, perhaps misunderstanding the profoundly ethical nature of the question, rather loudly expressed his support for the rival prisoner.

For the next five years of secondary education this immoral cur was contemptuously referred to as "Barabbas".

EVERY student of architecture knows that one of the great practitioners of the profession was Mies van der Rohe, who famously designed minimalistic buildings.

Reader Paul Boyle recalls Glasgow School of Art's house-cat in the early 1960s: "Meece van der Rodent".

IN the 1970s the Southside Division of the Edinburgh Police Force had a chief inspector called George who reinforced his refusal of requests by saying: "Ah, nut nut nut nut nut."

Geordie Nut Nut soon gained the nickname "The Rear Gunner".

FORMER policeman David Russell, from Penicuik, had a colleague who was cruelly referred to as "Wobble You" because he couldn't pronounce the letter R. American tourists seeking directions to Hollywood Road (which was actually Holyrood Road) were informed by this chap: "It's not Hollywood, it's Holywood."

Cue confused tourists.

ONE of the plumbers employed by George Dale from Beith had a reputation for overcharging on "homers".

Because of this he became known as the "White Spirit". The logic being that he was a bit of a robber, just like Dick Turpin. And Dick Turpin sounds rather like turpentine. Which is, of course . . . a white spirit.

OUR readers live devil-may-care lives. Their everyday existence is permeated with the grit of a Hemingway yarn and the glamour of an F. Scott Fitzgerald tale.

Though sometimes the Diary cynically wonders whether some of our correspondents stretch the truth, just a tad.

Case in point: a Hamilton reader tells us he once had his fortune read by singer Eddi Reader's sister, Pam.

THE English language is useful when it comes to matters of communication . . . and miscommunication.

We hear of a man of the cloth, very much above reproach, who had to catch an early plane out of New York. So, he told the receptionist he wished to be "knocked up" at 7 a.m.

NOVELIST Robert Wilkinson asks: "What did they call barn owls before barns were invented?"

Our guess is they were probably called "impatiently waiting for barns to be invented owls".

SOCIABLE Margery Dobson often stops to chat to fellow dog walkers, some of whom are runners.

She was once ambling across a field when she was greeted by a man, wrapped up against the cold, strolling with a friend. It took Margery a moment to recognise him as one of the chaps who usually went jogging in much skimpier attire.

Without thinking, she said: "Oh, hello. I didn't recognise you with your clothes on."

The fellow raised his finger to his lips and hissed: "Shhh! It's a secret."

"I'm about twice his age," chuckles Margaret. "You should have seen his friend's face."

ONE of the legal services on offer is a "police station visit", where a lawyer agrees to meet a prospective client detained by the Boys in Blue.

An elderly lady once phoned solicitor Matthew Berlow's firm, requesting such a visit.

As Matthew was in the process of enquiring what heinous crime the old woman was accused of – running amok with a knitting needle, perhaps? – she interrupted him.

"No, no," she said. "It's for my wee grandson. He's always wanted to see what goes on inside a police station, so he'd like one of your police station visits."

WE recently pointed out that our correspondents are adventurous types who would have gladly left home and hearth to participate in the California Gold Rush.

Alas, the only gold rush in modern times takes place during a bargain sale of trinkets in Glasgow's Argyll Arcade. Meaning our frustrated readers are sometimes forced to stretch the truth a tad when telling ripping yarns.

For example, a reader informs us: "I once met Peter Pan's brother, Algy."

WE continue shining a spotlight on the sadly forgotten relatives of celebrated worthies. Reader Larry Cheyne points out that many people enjoy the paintings of Salvador Dalí. He adds: "Personally, I prefer his sister, Dilly."

THE ambition of cultured reader Colin Hodges is to build an Oxymoron Museum. He says: "I'd have a civil war room, private exhibitions and permanent loans."

ANOTHER suggestion for our Oxymoron Museum from reader John Maclean. "There could be a gallery for Alloa Athletic," he says.

A PHILOSOPHICAL thought from reader Jay Harvey, who says: "A common mistake inventors make when designing foolproof gadgets is to underestimate the ingenuity of your average fool."

RACING aficionados were excited when the Cheltenham Festival galloped into view. The ever-generous Diary decided to help our readers become disgustingly wealthy by advising them which horses to back.

Our top tipster, and man in the paddock, was Sandy Tuckerman, who learned Horsish, the language spoken by all educated equines, while the rest of our readers were boning up on their French and German.

Here's the advice Sandy obtained from the gossiping gee-gees regarding who will cross the finishing line first.

1:30:	Leaky Tap – Though only if it's running.
2:10:	Foundation – You can put your house on it.
2:30:	Creosote – Great over fences.
2:50:	V Neck – A terrific jumper.
3:10:	Ironing Board – You can put your shirt on it.
3:30:	Dusty Rug – Never been beaten.

CLEARLY reader Alan Nicholson has too much time on his hands, as he gets in touch to say: "If you rotate the word rotator you get rotator."

IN the early 1960s there was a tradition in an Ayrshire hospital where junior medics would entertain staff with a short show at Christmas. Characters featured in the show were satirical versions of the genuine doctors.

So the respected surgeons Messrs Ralston and Sangster became Gallstone and Gangster while orthopaedic surgeon Mr Simpson was Mr Limpson.

A CONTEMPLATIVE thought from reader Maurice Thompson, who says: "Maybe tornadoes only run into things because they're so dizzy from spinning."

CONGRATULATIONS to the fiery young Airdrie writer Len Pennie, who has been named Poet Laureate for the St Andrew's Society of Los Angeles.

The Diary didn't even realise there was a Scots population in LA sizable enough to have its own St Andrew's Society. Then we recalled that famous resident of Hollywood, and star of such movies as *One Flew Over The Cuckoo's Nest* and *The Shining*.

How could we have forgotten Jock Nicholson?

TWITTER is a forum famous for its reasoned debates and precise, factual comments. For example, Sarah Vine, the estranged wife of cabinet minister Michael Gove, boasts on the social media site that she enjoys visiting Glasgow, especially its wonderful "Ubiquitous Fish" restaurant.

The Diary is eager to know if she has also strolled down the city's Squelchyhill Street, or visited its Mitchell Brothers Library. (Famous for holding the world's most extensive collection of *EastEnders* memorabilia.)

A CURIOUS reader wonders if Sarah Vine has also visited Pillock House, which is, of course, only a few steps from the Barrel Collection. (Sherry barrels, beer barrels, roll out the barrels . . . They've got the lot.)

A THOUGHTFUL Andrew Cathcart from Linlithgow points out that many fleshers advertise themselves as "First

Class Butchers". "Always wondered why the Second Class ones don't shout it from the rooftops," he muses.

CONCERNED reader Alan Potter gets in touch to say he was sorry to read about a recent accident on the M74, where a lorry spilled its cargo of onions.

He adds: "Presumably the emergency services went looking for a hard shoulder to cry on."

CONFUSED Sam Martin from Shawlands is trying to sniff out the truth regarding a linguistic conundrum, and asks: "Which letter is silent in the word 'scent'? Is it the S or the C?"

THE *Herald* reported that a woman has a twenty-stone pig living in her Carluke house. Ian Sommerville from Largs rather unfairly says: "Chap a few doors and I reckon more than one woman will convince you there's a twenty-stone pig curled up by her fire."

IN the 1960s Ian McDonald was an apprentice in a Glasgow engineering company. Among the people working there were two chaps called William Wood and David Cant. Inevitably a rumour began that Willie Wood . . . but Davie Cant.

THE above tale reminds a reader of two women he once worked with who were rumoured to be rather cold when it came to romance. Not because of anything they said or did.

Nobody ever discovered how Wilma Wilney and Nora Night got saddled with such reputations.

MEDICALLY minded Sid Leslie from Kirkintilloch points out that the right side of the brain controls the left side of the body while the left side of the brain controls the right side of the body.

Our reader adds: "Left-handers can take comfort from being the only people in their right minds."

A PHILOSOPHICAL thought from reader Colin Jarvis, who points out: "Intentionally losing a game of Rock, Paper, Scissors is just as hard as trying to win."

27

The Games People Play

JUST when you thought it was safe to go back into the voting booth a new political party appeared on the scene, with Alex Salmond's Alba Party playing Pepsi to the SNP's Coke. The rival tartan teams would probably hate that analogy as they both see themselves as Irn-Bru thru and thru.

The Alba Party was soon being subjected to criticism because of the calibre of its candidates. (To remind yourself about the problems they faced over the past year, flick back a few pages and reacquaint yourself with chapter two.)

How much scrutiny went into choosing Alba's team of hopefuls? It was hard to say.

That's not the case with the Diary, of course. We've always been clear and transparent regarding the box-ticking exercise developed to choose our contributors. First, we show potential candidates a photograph of a brush. Then we ask them a simple multiple-choice question. Are you:

(a) Less daft than this household implement?

(b) As daft as this household implement?

Candidates who answer (b) are invited to contribute.

To prove how majestically ditzy our successful candidates truly are, this chapter includes a generous helping of the madcap mind games they constantly bombard us with.

SCHOLAR of the Scots tongue, Paul H. Costello, gets in touch to warn us that confusion often arises when popular local phrases are used in a careless manner, especially when those phrases have several meanings.

He supplies us with the following examples to highlight this truly worrying problem . . .

Taps aff = It's lovely outside.

Taps aff = You're wasting water.

Taps aff = I'm not lending you any more money.

Get tay = Go away.

Get tay = We might need two.

Gies peace = Shut up.

Gieus piece = I want your sandwich.

Hod up = Ready to carry bricks.

Haudup = I might be home late.

Hoodup = It's raining.

Do wan = Go away.
Do wan = One will be sufficient.

Am sick of yoose = You're annoying me.
Am sick of ewes = I am fed up with sheep.

Nae mare = I've had enough.
Nae mare = Take the horse away.

IN a similar vein, our readers informed us they were very concerned upon realising that many famous Scottish locations can easily be confused with alternative meanings. Examples of this worrying sort of mix-up are supplied here.

Pollokshields = Fish waiting for vaccine.
Bothwell = Neither of us are affected by Covid-19.
Motherwell = The same is true of my parent.
Renton = We don't have a mortgage.
Carntyne = Traffic accident in Newcastle.
Killiecrankie = A hatred of women dressed as small schoolboys. (Or: The grumpiness of Kilmarnock FC fans at the recent performances of their team.)
Royston = Stay there, Roy.
Rothesay = That man talks rubbish.
Killearn = An advert for a hitman.
Ardlui = A Mafia enforcer.
Brodick = Fraternal eejit.
Oban = Attempt to reduce the alphabet by one letter.

Monifieth = An embezzler.

Kenmore = An unlikely occurrence when you have to home school during lockdown.

Aberlady = A female naturist.

Menteith = They're no falsies.

Portknockie = A suspicious noise coming from the left-hand side of a boat.

Pittenweem = Possible suggestion when a person fails to remember their log-in password correctly.

Lanark = French female informant.

Dundrennan = We have completed the waste-water disposal system.

Methil = A hangover from drinking cheap alcohol.

Abernethy = An unclad Loch Ness Monster spotted by a person with a lisp.

Dumfries = Speechless chips.

Torridon = A right-wing academic.

SOMETIMES Diary contributors have a more positive outlook when they get in touch. Instead of bombarding us with pesky problems, they help us out by providing much-needed solutions. For instance, our readers decided to devise advertising jingles, based on famous songs, to support local businesses and kickstart the economy. The following were suggested . . .

TOM Bain believes the local butcher shop should be promoted with 'Veal Meat Again'.

To give the optician an economic boost he suggests: 'I Can See Clearly Now'.

And for the bakery: 'What The World Kneads Now'.

CHRISTINE Brooks suggests Lana Del Rey should be hired to promote neighbourhood hairdressers by warbling: 'Born to Dye'.

ANOTHER reader believes The Beach Boys should promote the local joiner by singing: 'Wooden It Be Nice'.

ROBERT Hamilton from Bearsden suggests a variation on a song from *South Pacific* to help promote his local fishmonger: 'Salmon Chanted Evening'. Meanwhile, reader Harry Shaw points out that the same ditty could publicise the local plumber with the lyrics becoming: "Someone's chanty's leakin'".

ROBBIE Duncan believes the tune from the movie *High Noon* could be adapted to celebrate neighbourhood cafés.

The lyrics would, of course, become: "Doughnut forsake me, oh my darling." (P.S. Our reader assures us his name is Robbie Duncan, not Dunkin'. So there's no conflict of interest in this particular proposal.)

COLIN Findlay wonders if we got the lyrics to the above song wrong: "Given the sugar and fat content of a certain popular treat," he says, "I always believed the words were: 'Doughnuts cause acne, oh my darling.'"

CARL Williamson from Largs wants his hometown's famous ice-cream parlour to be celebrated by adapting an ABBA song, which would now be known as: 'Super Scooper'.

JOHN Mulholland suggests that neighbourhood stores specialising in children's games and playthings would witness a boost in sales by adapting the 1976 Thin Lizzy song: 'The Toys Are Back in Town'.

THE neighbourhood hosiery shop would receive a welcome increase in sales with the help of a classic Queen number: 'We Will Sock You'.

JOHN Little from Suffolk has an alternative idea to increase hosiery shop purchases by using the Moody Blues classic: 'Tights in White Satin'.

BERT Peattie from Kirkcaldy believes customers might be persuaded to leave McDonald's and instead visit a local sandwich shop with the aid of a classic Lennon/Ono number: 'Give Piece a Chance'.

ALTERNATIVELY David Donaldson says Scotland's Italian restaurants could do with some publicity, so suggests John and Yoko's hit would be put to better use as: 'Give Pizza a Chance'.

SHOE shops would receive an economic boost by using the 1967 Sam & Dave classic 'Sole Man'.

PUBLICANS keen to gain a trading advantage by advertising the delivery of kegs of fresh beer for thirsty punters should use the 1957 Buddy Holly classic: 'That'll Be the Dray'.

SHOPS selling bread and cakes might see a revenue rise by using a tuneful ad based on Gerry Rafferty's classic: 'Baker's Treat'.

GARDEN centres could see the green shoots of recovery with an advertising tune based on the catchy 1985 song by Billy Ocean . . . 'When the Mowing Gets Tough'.

THE Diary strives to float majestically above the humdrum and hurly-burly of modern life. That's why we avoid the daily news cycle, preferring to peddle jauntily on our trusty news penny-farthing. Are we too esoteric, perhaps? Too highfalutin?

Not at all. Indeed, we aim to provide our gourmet readership with the richest possible fare. Which is why we sometimes dabble in the Latin tongue, with our contributors reminiscing about their favourite verses in that splendiferous language . . .

VERONICA Liddell recalls a favourite ditty from her studies at St Mary's in Bathgate:
"Cedem lores
Cedem go
Forte lores in aro
Demarnt lores, demar trux
Fulla hensan causan dux."

JOHN Shedden from Perth was taught by a Latin teacher at Gourock High in 1958, who assured the class that the august language included the phrase: "Pitra per errum affrabus."

DAVID Gemmell from Latin-loving Lanark learned the subject in 1961. Furthermore, his wife, Louise, can recite a schoolgirl ditty about it:
"Latin is a language as dead as dead can be,
Latin killed the Romans, and now it's killing me."

WHEN Julie McAlpine attended Notre Dame High School in Dumbarton in the mid-1960s, her Latin teacher was a Miss Lorkin. Known affectionately as Lorky, she was immortalised in the following ditty:

"Lorkibus satisbus on the deskalorum
Deskibus collapsibus
Lorky's on the florum."

A GIFFNOCK reader was taught the sublime language in King's Park secondary school, where lessons included conjugations for verbs and declensions for nouns.

Our reader recalls that the Glasgow version of the conjugation of the verb amare (to love) was: "amo, amas, amat, amamus, adamus and a wee babymus."

SEVERAL readers recall that in the late 1950s and early 60s there was a Latin teacher at Greenock Academy, the much-respected Cameron Love. He happened to be a chap of small stature, which led to him being known as Amamus, which translates as We(e) Love.

BERT Houliston says there is an official football managers' conjugation of the Latin verb "dungood".

"I dungood; you dungood; 'e dungood; we dungood; youse dungood; that boy Andy Robertson, 'e dunbrilliant."

LINDA Mumphrey from Muirend recalls some useful guidance from her cousin Marvin: "Semper ubi, sub ubi."

About the Author

LORNE Jackson began his career as a diarist at a precociously youthful age. His parents bought him a blank notepad when he was seven and encouraged him to keep a record of momentous events, much as Samuel Pepys, the seventeenth-century English scribe, had done when bearing witness to the Second Dutch War and Great Fire of London.

The day after receiving his notepad, Lorne took a sabbatical from diary writing, realising the possibility of witnessing a Third Dutch War, or even a minor London blaze, were depressingly small from his vantage point in a Scottish council house. Besides, he didn't have time to pursue literary aspirations. He was too busy playing Tig with his pals.

In the ensuing years, Lorne worked as a feature writer, columnist and Jackson-of-all-trades, returning to his initial love upon assuming the fabled Herald Diary mantle. The secret he'll take to his grave is that *Herald* readers do the majority of work, feeding him amusing anecdotes. (Shh! Keep that to yourself. If anyone finds out, he'll lose his job and succumb, again, to a life of Tig.)